Love You More Than You Know

Love You More Than You Know

Mothers' Stories About Sending Their Sons and Daughters to War

edited by
Janie Reinart *and* Mary Anne Mayer

GRAY & COMPANY, PUBLISHERS
CLEVELAND

Photo credits appear on page 230.

A portion of the proceeds from sales of this book will be donated to ReMIND.org, a Bob Woodruff Foundation initiative for injured service members and their families. The Injured Marine Semper Fi Fund will also receive donations.

Gray & Company, Publishers
www.grayco.com

Library of Congress Cataloging-in-Publication Data
Reinart, Janie.
Love you more than you know : mothers' stories about sending their sons and daughters to war / Janie Reinart and Mary Anne Mayer.
p. cm.
1. Mothers of soldiers—Attitudes—History—20th century.
2. Iraq War, 2003—Personal narratives, American. I. Mayer, Mary Anne. II. Title.
HQ759.R459 2009
956.7044'38—dc22
[B] 2009012430

ISBN: 978-1-59851-055-3

Printed in the United States of America

10 9 8 7 6 5 4 3 2 1

To the two soldiers in my life,
my father, Joseph Vayo
and my son, Joseph Reinart

— Janie Reinart

To my son, Stan,
and to the memory of my grandmothers,
Anna and Franceska,
who sent their sons to war.

— Mary Anne Mayer

Contents

Love You More Than You Know

Introduction

Mothers are not prepared to let go when their children grow up and become soldiers.

For all of their young lives, we have fiercely protected our sons and daughters. We watched them sleep, gently touching their backs to make sure they were still breathing. We taught them to look both ways before crossing the road. We warned them to beware of strangers. We reminded them to wear a helmet when riding their bike . . .

But now that *they* have become the protectors, now that our children—proud servicemen and servicewomen—have left us to go to war, it will never the same again.

Now, we cannot protect them.

We still worry, but our worries are about mortar fire and IEDs. The helmets are worn in a humvee. The strangers they meet may be suicide bombers.

All we can do now is wait. We wait for an e-mail message or a letter. We wait for a phone call to hear the sound of their voice, just to hear them say "Mom." When we hear their voices, listen to their stories, maybe even see their faces on a videoconference from a foreign land, we know that, for that moment, they are safe. We string together those moments, word by word, like prayer beads, until we make it through a deployment.

This book, a collection of true love stories, bears witness to the heartache and joy, the fear and pride of mothers awaiting the safe return of their children from war.

The project started when two of us wrote our own stories and began speaking at military support meetings, inviting other mothers to write and share theirs. Writing our stories allowed us to make sense of our raw emotions, from our deepest fears to our greatest hopes. Sharing them bonded us to other mothers who were facing their own children's deployment, and we no longer felt alone.

After we collected a dozen stories, we contacted Cleveland *Plain Deale*r columnist Regina Brett. She graciously featured us in her column and on her radio show on WCPN FM, our local NPR affiliate. The response was tremendous; for months after the show, stories continued to arrive.

The stories came from ordinary moms with various backgrounds who all now share the common bond of service to our country. Celeste Hicks is the mother of five children, and not just one, but all five, are soldiers. Carol Sue Tengler sent an eighteen-year-old soldier to boot camp not knowing that twenty-two years later she would still be an Army mom. Both Lucky Caswell Harris and Saundra Hunt sent their daughters to war, and both started military support groups to fill a need in their communities. Noël Burr's daughters have dedicated their lives in service to our country. Her oldest daughter is a colonel in the Air Force Reserve and her second daughter is a lieutenant colonel in the U.S. Army.

These 45 stories together show, vividly and honestly, the reality of a mother's life during her child's deployment: The "shock and awe" of having our children enlist, train, and then be deployed. The dread of an unexpected phone call or a military car in our driveway bringing bad news. Addiction to the twenty-four-hour news stations. Endless hours of packing boxes to send to our troops. The joy of those short emails or phone calls from our soldiers to help us make it through another day. The inspiration and courage we draw from our soldiers to fight our own battles at home, from struggling with cancer to being widowed.

We lightened our burden by writing and sharing these stories. One mother confided that she carries her story in her purse everywhere she goes so that it is always with her. Another mom told how she cried the whole time she was writing, but when she was finished writing felt like she was finally starting to heal. Another mom waits for the moment her soldier returns home to present her story as a gift.

If you are on your own journey of separation from a child serving in the military, our stories offer courage and hope, showing you how we survived.

If you do not have a family member serving, these stories offer insight into what our troops and their families sacrifice everyday, because they fight for all of us.

We want everyone to remember and support our troops. One of our moms, Laurie Goyetche, described it best when she wrote, "They are young men and women who do not stand behind their flag; they stand in front of it, risking their lives for the American way of life."

To our mothers, we thank you for raising fine men and women willing to protect our freedom. To our children, we are deeply grateful, more than words can say, for your service, your gift to our country. And to those service men and women who have given life itself to protect us, the only thing we can say is, *We love you more than you know.*

—Janie Reinart and Mary Anne Mayer

Time Will Start Again

Amy Kenneley

THE CLOCK ON HIS bedroom wall stopped many months ago—I can't remember exactly when.

He hasn't been home since last Christmas, and my projects and hobbies have gradually drifted into corners here and there, like dandelion fluff. Summer clothes are crammed into his closet, where only his bathrobe had hung. Now, I am driven to clean and organize, to freshen the room, to put new sheets on the bed. An e-mail confirmed he's coming home.

Since February of this year, he has lived on an amphibious assault ship with several thousand other Marines and Navy personnel. He has been carried into battle on helicopters, has been driven miles into mountains in Humvees, and, for the first time, has known what it is to command under fire.

There have been endless frustrations and deprivations, and now, finally, a brief respite before being reassigned—because this is his life, his career. His boyhood room is just a brief stopping point before moving on again.

I wonder if this larger man will fit into this tiny room now. Surely it is bigger than the bunks aboard ship. Maybe the size of the room isn't what I should be measuring. Maybe he will tell us how he measured up out there in a very hard school of hard knocks.

I only have little bits and pieces, you see. Remember V-mail? Well, e-mail is the descendant of that super-thin, crinkly letter in pale blue that would arrive weeks, sometimes months, after it was written. Now messages zip through cyberspace across continents and oceans. Often in the early morning hours I would tiptoe upstairs, and with only the ghostly screen's gleam to guide me, I would sit in the dark waiting for a message to download. It was like a reassuring hug when I saw his name pop up. I could imagine him sitting somewhere hunt-and-pecking. I noticed he still misspelled the same old words, but it was reassuring to read them. To see the familiar wrongs seemed to make everything right—in the dark before the dawn.

Sometimes he sent photos: a stray dog the unit befriended in Mosul, lying in her own foxhole dug by the guys, or one of himself standing on someone's porch beside a large portrait of Saddam Hussein (I wonder how many others posed that day?). Mostly, he sent one-line messages—mundane replies to our mundane questions. As long as the messages came—frequently or infrequently—I knew he was okay.

Then for a while, we didn't hear from him. I kept the television on CNN, at first mesmerized by the video clips, then listening with half an ear for any familiar unit names. The mail came, and in the roadside mailbox was a piece of cardboard. I found out later it was the end flap from a box of Meals, Ready to Eat, or MREs.

One side of the cardboard had his name and military unit in the top corner and our name and address centered. Where a stamp should have been, he had written "FREE-OIF," and the postal authorities had dutifully acknowledged that stiff brown flap's right to free postage in a combat zone by postmarking it.

The familiar writing, scrawled across the bumpy corrugated

lines, told us he was okay. We passed it around in amazement to our children and friends, as though it was some kind of holy writing, when it was really just a piece of cardboard that had traveled halfway around the world to our little corner of Ohio. The message read,

> Dear Mom and Dad . . . I'm alive and well and currently in Northern Iraq. Have been here since 12 April in city of Mosul. I should be back on ship by the time you get this. Love, John.

I wondered where he was when he wrote it . . . maybe he will tell us when he gets home. I considered the many people who handled that piece of cardboard through the military and then the civilian mail systems. How many looked at it and read those lines? Did they wonder who we were and who he was, or just toss it into the mailbag? It continues to amaze us that something I almost threw away as trash, something with such a humble use as a meal container, could make it so far.

I am daydreaming as I dust and rearrange his room. I place front and center the scrapbook I have kept of his deployment: news stories, photos, e-mails, information and updates from his unit's website. And of course, in a plastic pocket, the brown MRE postcard.

So much has happened since he left last year. Perhaps he will never truly catch up with the local news or with national events. His sister taped rugby matches to mail to him. His sister-in-law baked cookies and sent him magazines. His brothers wrote to him or sent e-mail messages. Everyone wanted to let him know he hadn't been forgotten. But it isn't the same as him being here.

He has missed many family milestones. One brother was married. One bought a house. One started college at night. One nephew won a swim meet, and another started preschool, while a new one was added to the family.

I have worn a mother's service pin for months now. Meeting others who recognize its meaning makes me feel less alone. Perhaps I can safely put away the pin and retire the service flag that has hung in our dining room window. The red and blue has faded from the sun, perhaps faded as much as public interest in conflict on the other side of an ocean.

But concern never fades for those who have friends and loved ones "over there." Prayers never end for them, for their safe return, or for those who have died in service to their country.

On the day President Eisenhower was inaugurated, a reporter asked his mother, "Aren't you proud of your child today?" She replied, "I am proud of all my children—which one did you mean?" I always thought that a grand statement from her, and now I know how she could say it. Each child is so special, with special gifts and talents, how can a parent not be proud of each and every one? To have them nearby is a gift. To have them far away tears at you. Like President Eisenhower's mother, I am proud of all my children too.

The summer clothes have been emptied from his closet. Soon, it will be stuffed with all his uniforms and equipment. I wipe the desk one more time, straightening his deployment scrapbook where he will see it. What have I forgotten? Oh yes, a new battery for the wall clock. Time will start again when he comes through that door.

Amy Kenneley is the mother of five grown children and grandmother of five grandsons. A lover of books, she also worked at her local public library system. She volunteers at her local historical society and is active in several genealogy groups.

Boots to Ground

Janie Reinart

THE SWEET, MOURNFUL SOUND of taps honored my father's leaving, echoing in the cold December morning. The silence was shattered by a color guard firing a twenty-one-gun salute. Our country's flag fluttered as it lay draped over the casket of a hero, Joseph Vayo, a Navy veteran of WWII. Reverently, the color guard folded this bright symbol of freedom into a triangle. My son, Specialist Joseph Reinart, Ohio Army National Guard, stepped briskly forward to receive the flag. Turning to my mother, Joe said, "On behalf of the president of the United States of America, I present you with this flag for your husband's faithful service to our country. May God bless you, and I love you, Grandma."

Just weeks later, Joe was leaving. My son, my father's namesake, my hero, was being deployed to the Middle East to serve his country as a peacemaker. When he was little, I would bundle him up to face the world safe and snug. Looking into his bright eyes, I would say, "Make sure you wear your boots and jacket and hat!" I never imagined thinking, "Make sure you wear your boots and flak jacket and Kevlar helmet!" This time he was bundled up to protect the world and keep it safe. I had thought about sending my child away to school, away to a new job, away to be married, but never, never away to war.

Time stopped. Night ran into day. I took off my watch and put on a lapel pin, the kind that holds a small picture in a frame—a picture of my soldier boy in his National Guard uniform. I wore Joe's picture over my heart every day. Because of that picture, strangers would stop me at the store, around town, or at church and ask, "Is that your son?" I would answer proudly, "Yes, please pray for him and for the safety of all our soldiers." No one ever refused my request.

All my phone calls were forwarded from home to my cell phone. I did not want to miss a single call despite the eight-hour time difference between Ohio and Iraq. When I did happen to miss some calls from Joe, I saved the voice messages so that I could listen to his voice anytime I wanted to, during the long eighteen months of his active duty and deployment for Operation Iraqi Freedom. He would be in Iraq for one year starting when his boots touched the ground. Joe, twenty-two years old, went on active duty December 18, 2003.

Joe was part of the 216th Engineer Battalion, which shipped out from training at Camp Atterbury in Indiana, reaching Kuwait on February 17, 2004. Their mission was to help rebuild Iraq. In Kuwait, they would acclimate to the extreme temperatures and receive more training before moving on to their base in Iraq. It was in Kuwait that Joe had his wisdom teeth pulled. He sent me a picture taken a couple of hours later that day and I saw him in body armor for the first time. He wrote, "My chinstrap is a little crooked because my jaw is still sore from the extractions." I had pampered his four siblings with ice cream and cold packs when they had their wisdom teeth out. I was very sad that I could not do that for my soldier. The look in his eyes in that picture told me that he was changing.

In an e-mail dated February 24, 2004, from Kuwait, Joe writes:

Hi Mom and Dad,
I miss you. I have been on active duty for 3 months and 6 days. At 6 mths. I will have veteran's status, which is awesome. Everything is sandy and dirty—can't escape the sand in my mouth, ears, eyes, hair, shoes and clothes—it is the enemy. I miss everything about being home. This is an experience that will change me forever, more discipline then I have ever had.
It makes me realize how good we have it in the USA. I love you. Joe

Early one morning in the predawn light, just before the 216th went overseas, I found myself in a semiconscious state between sleep and wakefulness. A startling image filled my mind. The vivid picture was of a soldier in tricolor desert fatigues wearing a helmet. The soldier's head was down, so I couldn't see his face. Behind the soldier was an angel with broad white wings criss-crossed protectively around the soldier. The overlapping of each individual feather in those strong wings reminded me of eagles' wings when the bird stretches and soars high in the sky. The image stayed with me for the rest of the day. How I wished that I could draw! I was changing too. I was realizing that I had no control of the situation and could only lift Joe up to God. My heart sang, "He will raise you up on eagle's wings."

The convoy from Kuwait to Camp Speicher in northern Iraq took three days. The unit bounced around standing in trucks, traveling two hundred miles a day to make the six-hundred-mile trip. Joe was the unit's SAW (squad automatic weapon) gunner, positioned half in and half out of a Humvee, packing a .50 caliber machine gun and on the lookout for snipers. I don't know how he got to be such a good shot. When he was little, I would never let him play with guns. In an e-mail Joe said:

> I am doing okay. We made it through the convoy; it was the most crazy thing that I have ever experienced! We actually made a wrong turn and ended up in downtown Baghdad. The streets were crowded and very suspicious. The base that I am living at now is attacked almost every night by drive-by mortar rounds. It is weird to wake up to the sounds of explosion. I hope everything is going well. Got to run. Love you. Joe

To stay strong spiritually, on March 19, the Feast of St. Joseph, I made the commitment to go to mass every day and become a prayer warrior. My pastor, Father Dan Schlegel, always says, "When you don't know what to do—pray." I continually realized how much I needed God. To stay strong physically, I worked out every day, lifting free weights, walking, and doing some low-impact aerobics. At one point Joe e-mailed me, "I am strong because you are strong." We were strong for each other.

I soon became friends with the postal clerks at my local post office, and they always asked how Joe and his unit were doing. Sending my love in packages from home, I became an expert at packing boxes and began shipping two a week. Initial shipments were of baby wipes, insect repellent, candy and gum to soothe the throat, sunscreen, a handheld fan, lotion, Chapstick, and socks. Then Joe asked for food because anytime they left their barracks, the soldiers had to be in full body armor and gear. For lunch every day the soldiers had MREs (Meals, Ready to Eat). Sometimes it was just easier to eat what you had in your room, and not go out in the heat after work. So every week I would shop for groceries in Ohio to send halfway around the world—always buying enough so that my soldier could share. Joe made so many chocolate chip muffins from a mix that just needed water and a toaster oven that he became known as the Muffin Man.

Joe e-mailed:

Hi Momma,
The snickers bars are great. Send a lot of them. stuff like that and snacks and food. I am hungry. it is such a hassle to go to the chow hall it is like 5 miles away. Cereal would be good too—the little boxes. I love you mom and miss you will write soon. Love Joe

For Joe's birthday in April, I sent a "Party in a Box," including streamers, party plates, napkins, cups, candles, candy, and a banner that read HAPPY BIRTHDAY. I researched on the Internet what kind of cake had the best chance of surviving the extreme heat (temperatures 100–130 degrees) for the two weeks to twenty-one days it might take the package to arrive. An un-iced angel food cake was the answer. To solve the problem of frosting, I added a jar of hazelnut chocolate spread so that Joe could frost the cake when the package arrived at his barracks. I remember hearing that some of the mail planes wouldn't be flying because a certain area was a hot spot. In my naiveté, I thought "hot spot" referred to extreme weather conditions. I soon found out the real meaning—that the fighting was fierce and the area was just too dangerous to receive any mail.

Families with sons or daughters, husbands or wives in the military always dread the unexpected phone call or knock at the door for fear of bad news about their soldier. On his birthday, Joe called. I listened to the quiet agony in his voice.

"Mom, we were on a convoy and thought we were lost. We pulled off the road and another U.S. convoy went in front of us. We decided we weren't lost after all and hooked up behind that other convoy. We went down the road a few miles and the truck in front of me was blown up.

"Mom, that was supposed to be me. If we wouldn't have pulled off, my Humvee would have been destroyed. Mom, the young driver in the truck was the bravest person I've ever seen. He managed to stop the truck even though his legs were blown off below the knee. We put up a safety parameter and applied tourniquets and called in the medevac helicopters."

I listened and prayed that I would say something comforting as my son continued to tell how he was spared and lived to see his twenty-third birthday the next day.

Armed with a digital camera, I began taking random pictures of things all day long. I e-mailed Joe pictures of the sunrise, the snowdrifts in the yard, a cardinal at the bird feeder—anything that was part of a normal day here in the States. Wondering if I was annoying him, I asked if he wanted me to stop. He e-mailed, "Don't stop, you're the only one that sends me e-mails." I continued with pictures and e-mails through all the seasons that he was gone. I especially looked for images of beauty to counteract the colorless beige world where he was now living.

Watching the news obsessively, I learned about geography in the Middle East, about cities like Tikrit and Mosul, about extreme weather conditions and sandstorms, and about customs and beliefs of a different country. I hoped and prayed that I never would see my soldier's picture on the news. I had to stop watching the news because it was just too stressful.

The list of people who wanted to know how Joe and his unit were doing kept growing. Many people told me, "Sending updates on the computer puts a face on the war for me." Messages might include Joe's first reaction to the desert in Kuwait:

> Dear Mom and Dad,
> I awoke on the bus ride and was taken back by the vast light brownness on all 4 sides of the bus. Desert everywhere is wild. Things are decent. Got a shower today and we're resting until tomorrow. I love you very much, I think about you all the time. Love Joe

Or a new meaning to driving:

Hi Mom,
Things are hot here upwards of 100 degrees. The nights are usually crystal clear, and the stars seem closer. Occasionally a Blackhawk helicopter will thump into the stillness. I went on a convoy yesterday to Camp Airifjan, Kuwait, it was 70 miles both ways very bumpy and your butt hurts from bouncing up and down. The traffic is like you were in rush hour and some of the same rules don't apply—one that does is the biggest vehicle has the right away. A huge trailer tried to cut me off and I edged him back and blasted my horn at him. It is funny because road rage could be taken to a whole other level, considering we have machine guns with ammo.

Or a message to a friend:

I miss being home where I enjoy all the simple commodities of life. Here we use porta-potties and sleep in tents.

In July, Joe came home for his two weeks of R & R. He said, "There are only three things that are beautiful in Iraq: the sunrise, the sunset, and the faces of the children." It was amazing to see him—to hug him and just hang out with him. The hardest thing was taking him back to the airport when he was done with his two weeks—we knew what war was like now. I thought I was to take Joe to the airport, because my husband was out of town. My oldest son, James, saved me by having Joe sleep overnight at his place and by taking Joe for his flight. James said, "Joe and I talked and we were doing fine, until I saw the bumper sticker on the car in front of us. It said: HALF MY HEART IS IN IRAQ." With that James broke down in tears.

Joe had been in Iraq for seven months and had five more to go when I received this letter from my son. I carried it around with me for the rest of his deployment.

Dear Dad and Mom,

Today is August 9. Up until the past 6 months, I have lived my life naively and unaware of the reality of the world. I have seen life and death and that is the tip of the iceberg. Although I am not on a trail in the jungles of Vietnam or in some trench in France during the Second World War, I have seen enough to make me realize life should not be taken for granted. Living and coping have become a parallel term to myself and most of the people around me. My life has changed, and I have a long journey ahead, not just the next grueling 6 months in a combat zone thousands of miles away from the sanity of the United States, but the road of my life. I have learned and watched true friends be there for me, and watched others fade. One thing that remains certain in my mind is that family is like a cornerstone of a skyscraper. The support you have given me is second to none. I am more grateful for this than words can express. I love you both and the strong unit our family has become. I look up to you both for the people you are, and the people you've made us kids. Sometimes I want to cry out for help or breakdown and quit but inside me, instilled in my mind are the values and will to drive on that you taught me. My life as a juvenile definitely affected me in my adulthood, but underneath the layers I truly believe I am a good person and know what it takes to become an even better person.

I think a lot of nights, restless nights, of the days to come. I ponder and daydream of the good and the bad and the anxiety weighs on me like a ton of bricks. Will I make it back? Will I be so different from when I left? What will I do with my life? Will I be successful? Will I be happy? All I know that is certain is you, and I rely on that fact alone to get me through the sweltering reality I live in. I love you and cherish you for bringing me into the world, raising me, helping me along my journey through life. I look forward to brighter days of picnics, and card games, and golf and chess, and church and things that families do together. I love you deeply, more than you know. Your son,

Joe

When my soldier was away, it was like being lost in a crowd and searching and searching for a familiar face. Sometimes it felt like I couldn't breathe. Sometimes I had no words. Sometimes I was so restless, I just didn't know what to do. Night ran into day, and I would start over again. Praying and asking others to pray with me helped the loneliness.

I received this e-mail from Joe at the end of August:

Hi mom
The email [you sent me] is heartfelt. I miss you and love you. It has been very hard the past few days we lost two more soldiers from our company yesterday please do not tell anyone I am sure you will find out the details from family support but do not say anything until you are told. It is hard but we will come together and make it home. I love you and I will call you soon.
Love Joe

It was physically painful for me to attend the funeral of our fallen soldiers. My chest ached, my head hurt, and I couldn't stop weeping. Bringing food and attending the funeral didn't seem to be nearly enough, but sometimes it is all you can give.

The next time I saw Joe was in a teleconference at the armory in December. We could talk and respond in real time from in front of a TV. At the end of our ten minutes, Joe had a bunch of guys from his unit come in front of the camera and say hello. It was wonderful to see his face. I didn't feel much like celebrating Christmas that year. It was the anniversary of my father's death and things weren't the same without Joe at home.

I started sleeping in my office by my computer—when I did sleep. You become desperate to hear from your soldier. On the IM (instant messaging) system on my computer, I attached a sound to Joe's screen name—tahdaaa! Because of the time difference, it was often 2 or 3 A.M. when that sound would awaken me from sleep. Jumping off the couch, trying not to get tangled in the blanket, I would scramble over to the computer and try to type. My words weren't spelled right. I tried to type fast, with really funny results.

Joe typed, "What's the matter with you? Are you drunk?"

"Yes," I answered, "drunk with no sleep." (The funny part is that I don't even drink.)

By the grace of God, we made it through the year. Now all that was left was the six-hundred-mile convoy back to Kuwait. Our soldiers are most vulnerable on a convoy. Remembering what Father Dan said, I asked if we could have a three-day prayer vigil (the same days the 216th was on the road). Joe e-mailed:

> Hi mom,
> I got a medal today at a little ceremony we had. It was an Army commendation medal. The day I told you before changed to one day early so 3 days after tracy's [his sister's] bday. Well I gotta run I love you and miss you. Joe

I signed people up to pray every hour for three days. We started the first night at 9 P.M. in the chapel (5 A.M. in Iraq) and stayed all night, finishing up the first day with mass at 9 A.M. Every time I thought I could not stay awake, someone new came into the chapel to pray with me. We continued praying around the clock for the next two days at home. As it turned out, Joe was bumped from the convoy and got to fly out on the airstrip the 216th had repaired and extended. When Joe got to Kuwait his sergeant on the convoy said, "I can't believe we had no delays, no breakdowns, and no attacks!" Joe just smiled and said, "You had a lot of people praying for you."

Joe's homecoming was February 11, 2005, a wonderful Valentine's Day present. The other half of my heart was home. In the crowded cafeteria at a school in Youngstown, teary eyed, my mom presented Joe with my father's flag for his faithful service to our country.

It took me at least a year and a half to start feeling like my old self—finally exhaling—ready to laugh and do things with friends. I was changed and humbled knowing that our soldiers are sacrificing so much for us each day.

Joe (twenty-seven years old and a sergeant) completed six years of service in the National Guard. Honorably discharged, he's finished one year of a two-year commitment in the Individual Ready Reserve. My family and I continue to love, to laugh, to pray, and to be strong. We continue to trust in God as we wait to see if Joe's boots will hit the ground again.

A storyteller, educator, and freelance writer, Janie Reinart seeks ways to give people a voice to tell their own stories through prose and poetry. She and her husband, Ed, are grateful for their five children and two grandchildren. Most weekends, you will find Janie praying and singing with the choir at Holy Angels Catholic Church.

The Year Our Children Went to War

Mary Anne Mayer

UNTIL SEPTEMBER OF 1999, I did not even know a Marine. I had not yet come to appreciate this noble band of brothers who embodied honor, duty, and commitment. They were only the nameless faces of soldiers from books and movies. I certainly did not understand their culture and warrior ethos. Nor did I know what it meant to be the mother of such a man. I had no idea of what joining this sisterhood would mean to my life.

Then, in September of 1999, I came home from school to find a Marine recruiter sitting at my kitchen table with my son. Almost instinctively I knew this would change the course of all the plans we had for him—Stan, our sensitive, unassuming, yet erudite son who loved to write and draw, visit the art museum, and watch *Inside the Actors Studio* with me. I was so overwhelmed, I could not speak. I was choked up, and the recruiter, embarrassed for me, apologized and said he'd return at a later time. Return he did, and, despite my protests, Stan signed up for the Marine reserves.

Sending Stan to boot camp was like sending Daniel into the

lions' den. Three months later, in the sweltering heat of Parris Island, he was recognized as the honor grad of his platoon. We could not have been more proud. Six foot four, square-jawed and broad-shouldered, he looked like a Hollywood poster for the Marines.

Juggling college and the Marines, Stan was able to do it all. "Okay," I thought, "this business of being a Marine isn't so bad." And then, on September 11, 2001, all hell broke loose, and I got a reality check.

Every time units were sent to the Middle East, Stan felt cheated, while I breathed a sigh of relief. Two years later he held his ill, ninety-three-year-old grandmother and said, "Don't cry, Grandma, it looks like my unit won't ever go over." Three months later she passed away, and his unit received orders for Iraq. I have no doubt that she and my dad (who passed away before my mom) watched over him during his tour.

I cannot possibly describe what it feels like to send your child to war. It's a bizarre explosion of fear and pride, helplessness and strength, anger and acceptance. Surrendering, I placed Stan in God's hands, and asked our parish priest to bless him before he left for Iraq. As I placed the blue star in our window, I finally understood the hearts of all the mothers who had gone before me throughout history.

"Mom, don't be sad. This is what I have prepared for. This is why I am a Marine." As he said this to me the night before he left, I remembered the ten-year-old Stan who was so drawn to the idealism of the Knights of the Round Table, and I feared that the hell of war would forever change him.

On a bleak winter's day in January, we put on brave smiles and held flags and signs as the buses drove our sons to the airport. I remember that when the buses were out of view, mothers who were strangers only minutes ago stood together on the side of a slushy road in Brook Park, Ohio, embracing one another with one thing in common—helplessness. Later, that night, while making a cup of tea, I sobbed when I saw that the sugar bowl was empty.

"Mom," Stan said, calling from California, where the Marines prepared for war, "don't worry about me. I'm in a special unit called 'MAP.' I drive the brass around to their meetings—kinda like the Secret Service for the military." I felt as though a huge weight was lifted. I mean, how often does one hear of officers being killed? What he did not say was that MAP also stood for Mobile Assault Platoon—a specialized unit of handpicked Marines who executed offensive missions against the insurgents. What I did not know was that while I was teaching junior high, or mopping the floor, or grocery shopping, Stan was watching a good buddy lose his leg to an IED (improvised explosive device) just one Humvee ahead of his. Or that he was writing a war journal, chronicling the conversations of his brothers sometimes days before they got wounded or killed. What I did not know was that rounds of ammo whizzed by his helmet on any given day, and that before each mission, the men in Stan's Humvee would recite the 91st Psalm because they were always in harm's way.

Our rituals get us through each day. I left Stan's leather jacket hanging on the back of the dining room chair—just as he had left it. There was always a vigil candle on our mantel, with Stan's picture carefully placed between a framed print of *The Good Shepherd* and a photograph of my mom and dad. No matter what I was doing or where I went, an enameled yellow ribbon with the Marine insignia graced my left shoulder. We wound a giant yellow ribbon and bow on an ancient oak in my daughter's yard. Alex, my two-year-old granddaughter, would frequently yell at their resident squirrel to leave it alone. "Go away, Mr. Squirrel, that's Uncle Stan's bow!" I began attending daily mass and saying the rosary for all the soldiers. Who would better understand the suffering of our troops than Mary, who stood and watched the Passion and death of her son?

The passing of each day, each week, each month, became a milestone. Then, on Saturday, May 7, 2005, I paused briefly by the mantel and gently touched the photograph of my dad. "Happy Birthday, Dad," I said. "Watch over our boy for me." Little did I know the danger my son was in that day. Little did I know that in a place called Haditha, Stan's Humvee was hit by a suicide bomber driving a white Ford Econoline van packed with explosives. As his Humvee exploded, Stan looked death in the face. Once the dust had settled, somehow Stan stumbled out of the driver's side and miraculously got up from the earth, entirely blackened by the explosion. As skin melted off his face and arms, he continued to return fire while trying to tend to the wounded. Stan carried his dead brothers to safety and held his corpsman in his arms as his eyes rolled back in the last fleeting moments of his life. One by one, in the milliseconds of combat, in the heat of hell, "Doc" Weiner, Cepeda, Marzano, and Graham all died. Out of seventeen men, four died and five were wounded at Haditha that night. All this while I dusted and vacuumed.

"God, let Your will be done. I got no control here." That was how Stan and his brothers had begun to pray—not to be kept safe from harm but to do His will. I was more selfish with his life. *I* wanted him! As I thanked God that Stan was spared, my heart cried for those mothers who, on Mother's Day, received the news that their sons were badly wounded or killed at Haditha. That Sunday afternoon, May 8, shaken by the reality of war, my family made our annual Mother's Day visit to the cemetery. As I touched the cold marble marker, I whispered, "Thanks, Mom and Dad."

I wish I could say that the war went away after May 7. But, tragically, the following five months continued to bring the war home to Columbus and Cleveland, with forty-nine of our brave sons having made the ultimate sacrifice as members of the 3rd Battalion, 25th Marines. My hands froze on the steering wheel and my legs began to shake when I heard on the radio that fourteen

Marines from Stan's unit had been killed on August 3. We rushed home and sat by the phone, praying that it would not ring and fearful of the sound of cars coming up the driveway. In the weeks that followed, funeral homes swelled with people paying their respects to more of Stan's fallen brothers. Funeral entourages with honor guards stretched for miles, and both the young and old stood at silent attention as the hearses passed by.

By the end of August, I had no more tears, but the solitary image of the mother of one of Stan's fallen brothers will forever remain in my mind. Grief-stricken, she sat on a stone bench in the garden of St. Albert the Great Church, in front of a statue of the pietà—in front of Mary holding the lifeless body of her son in her arms.

Under the blue skies of a warm October day, the members of the 3rd Battalion, 25th Marines returned home to a hero's welcome in Brook Park, Ohio, as hundreds of people lined the streets—a testament not only to those who returned home, but also to those who did not. The auditorium where families and friends gathered pulsated with excitement as we anxiously awaited our sons' arrival. I felt physically lighter than air, and when I finally reached Stan, I wanted to hold him forever.

In the ensuing months I would sometimes just look at him while he slept—just like I used to do when he was born, just making sure that he was really there, that he was all right. Lying there, he looked the same. The physical wounds of war had healed. But he didn't do a lot of sleeping. He seemed distant. The war did not end with the October bus ride. Talking about mundane things was awkward for me, yet that was all that Stan wanted to talk about. Stan became a spokesperson for his unit, and, little by little, through his interviews and speaking engagements, published magazine articles and the photographs he had taken in Iraq, I began to get a clearer picture of the war. But I needed only to look into his eyes to know that there are stories I will never hear.

While Christmas shopping that year, I came upon a painting of an angel embracing a soldier with his wings. The 91st Psalm was superimposed in the desert background. "Could you please wrap this up for me?" I asked the clerk, as I fought to hold back tears. This Christmas gift for Stan could say what I could not put into words. This angel could bridge the awkward gap I felt, because I knew that, though I was Stan's mother, this war was something that on many levels I could not share with him. This beautiful psalm, sung thousands of years ago near the same hills where the war was now being fought—this, Stan would understand.

We are all changed forever by events larger than ourselves. We must go on, but we will never forget the year our children went to war.

Mary Anne Mayer became an Army wife when she joined her husband, Stan, at the Arctic Test Center in Fort Greely, Alaska. She has degrees in theater and secondary education, and she teaches art, religion, and writing, and co-directs plays, in junior high school. She and Stan have three children and delight in being grandparents.

Perchance to Dream

Mary Jane Kashkoush

I WILL BEGIN AT THIS point in time, July 23, 2008, looking in my rearview mirror, as I'm still wavering. Today is the eighteen-month anniversary of my beloved son Michael's leaving this earth. I must recalibrate the form—the direction my life will take, because this blow is crushing. I am not able to separate the "him" and the "I," so the secret symmetry of survival has to be forging ahead with an ancient spirit—faith—like being in a tornado with an umbrella.

My son, Michael, started his military endeavor in a sixteen-week boot camp regiment with the Marine Corps at the recruiting station Parris Island, in South Carolina, from January to April 2003, culminating with his graduation. We reunited at the ceremony filled with great pride.

He worked in a computer and communication center in Norfolk, Virginia, receiving and directing computer messages. He was then chosen to be one of approximately 180 elite Marines to study counterintelligence (CI) at Norfolk.

I take one day at a time and try to just get through it. I don't even approach why—a spiritual matter as vast and mysterious as the ocean I revere—I just wade in.

My love connects the lyrics of Steve Winwood's "Arc of the

Diver" to the image of the CD lying on Mike's bedroom floor. I draw on the comfort of these two images intertwined: one the effortless grace of the diver's descent to earth, and the other, Mike listening to it, enjoying life!

In 2005, he received a call telling him that he was chosen to study Arabic at the DLI (Defense Language Institute) in Monterey, California, and he drove across the country to live there for the next eight months. In August, he was assigned to a team of eight based in Okinawa, Japan. Mike would be one of those specialized Marines in small units doing CI work while traveling with an eight-hundred-troop Army battalion as an Arabic translator.

Grieving is a solitary road, but mothers in particular seem to bridge the distances created by loneliness and heartache. My friend Harriet told me, "You have no choice," and her tender intention got through beyond the literal, stark statement. Another year—wow, staying busy. I made it! I have survived the unbearable, how? I survived because of my sister's daily phone calls—even with the silence following one of us speaking of Mike. A friend had given her a phone to use just for this purpose—so sweet. This carried me through the winter, spring, and summer.

As the first warm weather came, I walked every day, my thoughts being with my Mike. There was a proliferation of monarch butterflies, unlike I'd ever seen since I was young—they were his messengers. I'm learning to relate. I try to retrieve something of value from each day, a treasure—a shell from my walk at the Headlands beach front today, or the image of a blue heron traversing the sky as I drove home. I embrace endless natural life, whose images evoke a connected oneness through time between this place and the other side.

Mike learned of the plans for his unit to go to Iraq in September, when they had to return to California for a three-week training program in the desert. I learned in December of 2006 that they would be deployed. Mike would be flying out on January 2, 2007.

Different day, same lingering feelings, like guests you wish would leave so you could go to bed—to sleep and perchance to dream. I imagine yesterday in the meadow of a memory: walking hand in hand, collecting flowers, Mike skipping a stone and making a ripple, observing nature at her morning best, playfully warm, sublime through all time. I juxtapose images from today onto a turtle hiding under its shell like the one Mike once caught with his "eagle eyes"—net in hand in a paddle boat. I feel reborn when he visits me in my dreams; they sustain my spirit until another rendezvous.

Mike's last e-mail, via BlackBerry, came to me in mid-January. He said their unit would be two days at their base, followed by three to four days in a local village on foot, talking to and surveying the locals. I've since learned that they were only two city blocks away from their base, returning after having left an Iraqi police station where Mike had translated. Their unit was walking through a marketplace when gunshots rang out. A sniper hit Mike. He was transported by his comrades to a medevac helicopter, then to a hospital. Although he was conscious up to the transport leaving, the severity of the injury was too great. Surgeons worked on him, trying to repair his internal wounds, for up to an hour.

The days to come seem daunting. I pray every night for less fatigue, and that in the morning I'll have more energy than the day before, as I just try to get through it. This process of grieving and reconnecting to life is like trying to tune in to a station on a car radio, the dial-in-knob kind, with static coming over the airwaves.

The world as I know it feels overwhelming and empty, like a dance for which I have no partner. As I turn my back on the sun I move forward, my faith in Mike fortifying me, by putting some tangible belonging from him in my pocket, like a talisman to give me his power.

How courageous and brave my beautiful soldier, warrior, and protector of the highest calling. For now, I'll reconcile by grounding myself in the ordinary business of every day, while I transform the extraordinary virtues of Mike's life and service into my service to others, helping those traveling a similar mom-and-son path. I hope to help them know they are not alone and must hold on.

My outlook has always been affirmative. I was trying to fit some remnant of my old life into the new one, but the circumstances wouldn't allow me to hide in a mock shell of my former self. This must be my dark night of the soul. As I learn to live with uncertainty always around the proverbial corner, this feels like a tidal wave. I hold fast, hold true to the absolute anchor in a relative sea, my undying love of my Mike. I've learned to take more in stride by reading spiritual books, realizing the temporal state of everything, that it doesn't last—it passes. My heart aches, but my instinct carries me through this trial, this matrix of sorts. Home is where the heart is, and my Mike is always with me.

EDITORS' NOTE: Sergeant Michael Kashkoush was awarded the Purple Heart posthumously. On May 7, 2008, President Bush signed Public Law 110-224, naming the Chagrin Falls Post Office in honor of Sergeant Michael Kashkoush. The legislation was sponsored and introduced by Congressman Steven C. LaTourette and Senator George Voinovich.

Mary Jane Kashkoush was born in Buffalo, New York, and currently lives in Ohio, but she has fond memories of Gerrards Cross, an ex-patriot town in England, twenty minutes northeast of London. Mary Jane belonged to the "American Ladies" group there that helped her assimilate into British culture. She fondly remembers tooling around town with Mike in their light blue BMW Z3 convertible, blaring favorite tunes, and driving on the right side of the road.

Time Out

Cindi Finnerty Condol

MY SON IS A captain in the United States Army, and his name is Padriac R. Finnerty. He served two tours of duty in Iraq, the second of which was extended twice. His first time over was in 2004. I watched, listened to, or read every story on television or in the newspaper. I would read the paper in the morning before I went to work to find out anything I could about what was going on over there that day. At lunch I would eat in front of the television and listen to what had already happened. Then after work, I would go home and watch the evening news to see how the day ended and who lost their lives.

I have a demanding job that requires my attention, but there were days when I would sit in front of my computer and just cry. Not a boo-hoo cry, but tears incessantly running down my cheeks. I would be dazed for a few minutes thinking about my son being over there and not knowing what he was going through. Sometimes, a coworker would walk over and say, "Come on, let's take a walk." Then we would just walk to the bathroom so that I could dry off my face.

On his first tour of duty he was a tank platoon leader. They were based in Balad and the surrounding areas. Every day on the news, you would hear of roadside bombs and how the troops were being attacked. It was a nightmare. I literally thought that I was losing my mind; I had no control—over my emotions or what might happen to my son. The wonderful, intelligent little boy that I gave birth to was over there, not only trying to fight off the insurgents and keep himself alive, but also responsible for many other men and their lives.

He called home as often as he could (which wasn't often enough) by way of a satellite phone or a calling card phone booth. But his conversations were always delayed, and sometimes I could swear that someone else was on the line. He always made me laugh. He would start out by yelling "Momma!" and I would scream his name back at him, "Paddy, Paddy is that you?" Then the tears would start, but I tried to hide them from him. I knew there was much too much on his mind, and I didn't want him to worry about me. Although I would find myself asking all kinds of questions about what was happening over there, I knew he just wanted to know how everyone was here at home. So, each of us got a little of both.

Men handle things very differently from women. My husband ignored most of what was happening, or at least that's how I saw it. I would get mad at him for not reacting to something that was on the news, or I would sit there and cry and he ignored it. He did not comfort me. When I did talk about how much this was hurting me, he would simply say, "Then don't watch the TV" or "Don't read the paper," as if it was my choice how I felt. He would also say, "Not everything they say is the truth." This put such pressure on our marriage that what happened next was not a surprise to anyone.

It was two weeks before our anniversary. I asked my husband to take the weekend off so that we could just get away for a few days. He moaned (like most men), then just said, "I don't want to; it isn't a good time." I told him I really needed to get away from it all . . . life, the war, my job, and the tension in the house. He just wasn't cooperating, so I did the next best thing. I left him!

On the day of our anniversary, I just left him. The pressure of it all just broke me. I was raised a strong Catholic girl who took care of everything—my family, my friends, my church, my job, and my house. I just couldn't do it anymore. The war broke me. I didn't know who I was, I couldn't mother my son, and I couldn't bear my husband. No one understood my pain. So, for my own sanity, I just called everyone I knew and told them, "Come now, I need help!" I was out of the house before he got off work. I moved to a little rental right down the street. I set up house and started to take care of me.

The hardest thing was to tell my son; I didn't want to waste the little time we had talking about my problems, but I was afraid that someone else would say something and that Paddy would misunderstand. So I told him. I explained it as a "time-out." I just needed to be alone for a while. I was fine, and Dad was fine, and we would all be fine again. I know my son was worried, but through our conversations we knew that all of us would be all right.

I kept everyone updated on what was going on with Paddy. I would send monthly messages, many with pictures that Paddy sent through e-mail. Many of my son's friends would respond with "Thanks, and our prayers are with you."

One night I got an e-mail from another soldier, a guy with whom my son went through ROTC. We "talked" a few times before he asked me a question that changed things for me; he asked me if his mom could e-mail me. She had been having a rough time while he was overseas as well. I said, "Sure." I met his mom via e-mail. Each day that we talked, we would cry. It was so overwhelming that each of us knew the pain the other was going through. It was a turning point for both of us and our sons. We have gone to each other's homecoming parties for our sons. We smiled and hugged and thanked God we had each other during those rough times.

After his first tour of duty, Paddy came home on leave, and by then my husband and I were, for lack of a better word, "dating." I know it sounds silly, but it helped. We had been separated for four months, but we never stopped loving each other and always knew we would be back together. It was time to leave the rental and go home. We let Paddy stay at the rental during his leave; this gave him some privacy. We all had a wonderful visit.

When Paddy was stationed in Germany, he changed his unit and his branch of the Army. He was now a platoon leader in the Quartermaster Regiment. His unit got called up, and in 2006 he found his way to Baghdad. The old feeling of panic started to resurface, and I found myself again getting lost in the war.

I had many talks with my husband, family, and friends. This time communications were much better. My husband and I talked often. We talked as if our son was at work out of town, doing a great job. It was easier to think of it that way. We got a little creative on how to handle everyday life, the news and government issues. We realized that we couldn't go through all that we did the last time. This time it was better. I wasn't doing it alone. In Baghdad, Paddy was able to call home more often. My husband and I would get so excited and ask him questions about his work and what they had accomplished. It gave us a more positive outlook on the war.

Our son just completed his military obligation and came home in February, just before Valentine's Day. It has been wonderful having him home. He is engaged and we are planning a wedding for November 2008.

My heart goes out to all who are still struggling with the pain, the separation, and the loss of their loved ones, and those still bravely supporting our right to be citizens in this free country. God bless them all, and may God bless America.

Cindi Finnerty Condol works as an assistant chief cashier and in-house auditor for her local county clerk of courts. She and her husband, Daniel, are active members of their parish, St. Malachi, and enjoy local Irish functions and traveling.

Be Not Afraid

Gloria Frombach

It was R-Day at West Point. The year was 1997. Reception Day is the day the plebes, or freshmen, begin their four-year journey at the United States Military Academy. The new cadets had just spent their first day getting measured for uniforms, receiving shaved haircuts, and enduring the constant shouting of orders from upperclassmen. At the end of the day, with new uniforms, the plebes marched past their parents onto the Plain to rounds of applause. As the new cadets finished their pass and review and all were standing at attention, the heavens opened and torrential rain and dangerous lightning came forth. The soldiers continued to stand at attention while the blinding rainstorm and winds ripped across the Plain, but no one moved until the order was finally given for them to be dismissed. My son, Matt Frombach, who at that time was in his second year at the academy, later told me that there was a superstition at West Point that if it rains on R-Day, that class would go to war. These new cadets would be the graduating class of 2001.

The United States was at peace. I knew when I left Matt at West Point that summer that he had signed himself over to the U.S.

Army. I cried all the way back to Cleveland, but at the same time I was so proud I could hardly stand it. And after all, we were in peacetime.

So, we went through the "West Point experience," as they call it. Our son brought his friends home occasionally for a weekend to meet us and see our fair city of Cleveland, Ohio. We loved all of them, and we were sure that each and every one of them had a bright future. At that time, we had no idea that in the real future, at least one of them would pay the ultimate price for our country. How could we imagine that eight years, later this handsome young friend of my son's would be kidnapped, along with four other soldiers, from a compound in Karbala, Iraq, and murdered in a war that no one could even begin to foresee?

After Matt's graduation from West Point, he was stationed at Fort Rucker, Alabama, for flight training. While stationed in Alabama, he qualified to fly the Army's Apache attack helicopter. He always wanted to be a pilot, and now his dream was coming true. I kept wondering where he got his wanderlust. Certainly not from me; I was the most overprotective mother on the face of the earth. And now I am the mother of a soldier? A pilot? I can't protect him. What will I do? So when Matt put a bumper sticker on his refrigerator that read, "Don't tell my mom I'm a pilot; she thinks I play piano in a cat house," I had to laugh and try to accept his decision.

When September 11 came, I can't even begin to tell you my feelings. I couldn't talk. My mother called me, crying. She said, "Matthew will go to war. You don't remember Pearl Harbor, but I do; this is the same thing, and Matthew will go to war." And I knew it was true, and I bowed my head and wept until I couldn't breathe.

On November 6, 2007, my son, Captain Matthew Frombach, deployed to Iraq as a commander with thirty pilots and mechanics in his charge. He left behind his wife of two years, Karen, and a sweet four-month-old baby girl, Isabel. I told Matt when he left that he shouldn't worry, that his family would take care of Karen and Isabel. His job was to stay focused, do his job, and come back to us.

Before Matt left for Iraq, he asked me not to watch the news. I don't, and I don't read the paper either. It is very difficult to avoid headlines; they are everywhere—in the stores, on CNN at work, on the radio, and almost everywhere I go. I have finally settled on watching the Weather Channel on TV—it is safe for me to watch (no headlines). I am becoming especially knowledgeable about hurricanes.

Sometimes both Karen and I have to endure angry comments by people against the war, and some of the things they say are completely inappropriate. The strange thing about it is that people actually think they are helping us feel better with their negative comments. Needless to say, it is very difficult for me to hold my tongue when our military is fighting so bravely for our country.

Sometimes I will just start to cry. I cry a lot. I am so grateful for dear friends and coworkers who are there for me when I come unglued for whatever reason. Sometimes I take to my bed for hours and pray. This usually happens when I accidentally hear something on the news like "fifteen killed in Baghdad," or "chopper crash." It doesn't matter if it is in a place my son wouldn't even be; I am still sure it is him. Despite all my worries, I must say that God has been faithful. Whenever I get in this state, either I will soon get an e-mail from Matt, or his wife will call and tell me she has heard from him. Karen is so good about letting me know right away whenever she hears from him, and I love her so much for that.

So, how do I shake my depression? I stay busy beyond belief. I work full-time at a police department. I can't even begin to think of retiring, even though I am eligible, because my job keeps my mind busy, and I have the best coworkers in the world who give me constant support.

I was disappointed to learn that we did not have a military support group in our community or at my church, so I began to pray for guidance to start one. After I announced plans for a support group around town, a woman I had never met, Laurie Weigelt, called me and said her son was in the Air Force. She wanted to be involved, so we met at a local coffee shop and prayed for people to show up. They did. Since we met eighteen months ago, we have gotten approximately twelve to fifteen active members and have completed three successful projects for our troops and their families. I learned something very important. I learned that no matter what opinion people have of this war, they dearly love our troops. And I was so proud and happy to share that fact with my son. Americans are opening their pocketbooks and praying for men and women in the military that they don't even know. This means the world to me and to all of our troops.

I am making patriotic bracelets to give to friends who have family deployed. When I am beading, I leave my worries behind and enter my own little world. My sister bought me a gold charm, the yellow "Support Our Troops" ribbon. I wear it on a chain around my neck, and I will continue to wear it until Matt returns.

Matt's story has yet to be told, because he is still deployed. When I talk to him, he says everything is great. If he confides in anyone, I am sure it is his older brother. He would never worry his wife, his sister, or me. It breaks my heart when I see Karen and Isabel at all the family gatherings, just the two of them, keeping on. Isabel celebrated her first birthday July 6 and is walking. Matt has yet to come home on leave, but hopefully will do that sometime in September. His tour of duty will end in February 2009. Until then, I will stay very busy and pray a lot. Sometimes I go to my husband's grave and ask him to watch over Matt. Sometimes I ask my mom, who has since passed away while he was deployed, to take care of Matt. But mostly I try to put my faith in God, who has allowed our family to come to this place. I believe He is doing a great work in all of us. Matt has things to learn in the desert, and we have things to learn here.

The title of this essay is the Bible verse that Matt chose to read at his baccalaureate service when he graduated from high school in 1994. None of us knew at that time how appropriate that verse would become for Matt and for all of us. I sign all of my e-mails to him with Psalm 91 (the Soldier's Psalm) and Joshua 1:9. I never thought that in my lifetime that I would be the mother of a soldier who is at war, but here I am. I am so incredibly proud of Matt, but at the same time I am scared to death for him. I am living on faith, prayer, and the love of my family and friends. I only wish I could be half as brave as my son.

Gloria Frombach's job as a police chief's secretary is never boring. She and her late husband, Ron, were blessed with three children and eight grandchildren. She loves crafting, cooking, designing things on the computer, and making cherry brandy—just for medicinal purposes, of course!

Learn That Poem

Eileen K. Lynch

I SOMETIMES PONDER THE MIKE-AND-DANNY incidents, situations, shenanigans, and what-have-you I survived. It gives me comfort to look at the photos of the boys growing up. I smile when I remember the many times I wanted to clock their noggins into the next century. Then I come to the photos when Mike graduated from Navy boot camp twelve years ago. I think about the words from the *Little Rascals* episode where Breezy Brisbane was haunted by his assignment to learn that poem . . . learn that poem . . . learn that poem. The story represents a life-changing moment for a naughty boy, a lesson he must learn, and a poem he must master and recite, no matter what. I was experiencing something life changing and soon realized that life was presenting lessons I would have to learn. I could only hope that I would develop Brisbane's humility, courage, and determination to learn and recite a new poem.

The first thing I felt was relief over the fact that the high-risk car insurance rates we were paying on a child who totaled two cars within one year (and he wasn't even driving one of them) were gone. The next thing I remember is the look on his face, his whole affect, when we said goodbye: I'm a man and I'm off. One week later I got what we Navy moms call The Box in the mail. In it were the clothes he wore the day he left, tossed in as if it was his bedroom floor. It hit me hard. I sat on the floor with the box, heartsick, and cried. In 1996, most folks I knew did not understand our family composition and the selfless sacrifice Mike was making. Some acquaintances were amused and queried, "What's the big deal?" Others thought Mike was not bright enough to do anything else. I had two daughters in college, and Mike's choice to follow a different path was a lonely one.

Boot camp wasn't anything like having a kid away at college. He could not call home at midnight to say, "You don't get much sleep and you sometimes have to stand watch in the compartment all night." I could not bring him home when he wrote, "I love all of you so much and miss my old life back home." If my child were injured, I could not fix it, hold him or sit at his side. Instead I could only hold on to his letter: "I could use some prayers . . . My feet ache so bad it is unbelievable, but I just face it . . . I also don't think about my feet and the ache goes away." I was beginning to learn the poem. In this verse, feeling proud of my son and honored to be his mother ran concurrent with heartache and rejection.

There are many things I could tell you about Mikey's service in the Navy, but that is for another day. He became a petty officer in the Seabees (the construction battalion of the U.S. Navy) and was honorably discharged in the spring of 2001. Mikey was and is a very strong man who acts fearlessly even when he's afraid yet his soul is gentle, compassionate, and loving. He survived sniper fire in Honduras and bar brawls in Korea and in his spare time provided a chicken dinner, real milk, and a baby doll for a little orphan girl on Christmas Day 1999. One more verse was added to the poem. It was about counting my blessings more and complaining less.

Following in his brother's footsteps, my youngest son, Daniel, left for boot camp in 1998. He too wanted to be a Seabee. Yikes!

One son was enough! Danny was a Boy Scout, honor student, gifted track runner, and college bound. Always fun, always creative, always charismatic, he suffered us with his larger-than-life ego. He wanted adventure and more, always more. I let go again. The weekend of his boot camp graduation was the weekend *Saving Private Ryan* was playing at the movie theaters, and the boys were dying to see it. Talk about tormenting Mom! I valiantly went to the theater with Danny and sat through the movie covering my eyes during the battle scenes and fearing I would soon be like Mrs. Ryan, hoping to save her youngest son. Please understand that during the 1990s and early in the new millennium, most military folks did not have Internet access or cell phones and could not call home whenever they wanted to. The only sure way to communicate with our children overseas was to write letters, mail them, and wait, wait, wait for a reply.

I mastered the poem and walked through the recitation, one day at a time. Then in a flash, everything changed; it was September 11, 2001. The horror and fear I felt went beyond what was happening in the United States. I felt the impact of what this meant on the world stage. Danny was in Korea and I hoped he would call home. I waited by the phone while harsh thoughts ran rampant through my mind. If the United States went to war, Seabee battalions like his would be the first to go, along with the Marines. I thought about the Vietnam era, and about the nearly two thousand Navy ground forces killed in action. I then remembered my youth, hopping on the protest train, clutching the words of the great poets—Arlo Guthrie, Country Joe & The Fish, and Jimi Hendrix. How did I manage to come through that purple haze intact and complete the transforming journey into motherhood, trusting God, and pride in America? I sat and I grieved over everything that had happened, everything that was presently happening, and everything that was about to happen. Sometimes learning the poem is a convoluted task.

It's difficult to go on from this point. Instead of embracing the therapeutic value of finishing this story, I'd rather shut down and defer the rest to my sweetheart, Danny's father. He was my rock, my voice of reason, my partner, and my passion. It no longer matters that at times he was my worst enemy. I wanted respite and downtime, and I wanted my husband back! How did we wind up with a patriotic kid? Why did the son we thought most likely to never seek a military career re-enlist? What was I thinking when I signed the permission papers for him to enlist? When is that damn kid going to call? Who is in charge of this whole thing anyway? With that, my Rolodex brain seizes. I know who's in charge of the universe and it's not me. I don't need those questions answered. I need to find a whole new set of questions, ones that bring peace.

I did get a reprieve when Danny returned from Korea. Instead of going to war, he stuck around in the States. He became an instructor, teaching new Seabees the building skills they would need for their deployment to the Middle East. Midway through 2003, Danny's orders took him to a communications base in the mountains of West Virginia. This was great! He was close enough to come home on long weekends. It was a godsend to have him close to home when my husband, Dan, got sick. His illness was a difficult battle for us all. The children were very close to their father and they all believed they were Dad's favorite. Each child was devastated in his or her own way, especially Danny. We all had to learn a new poem about grieving and then moving on.

During his assignment in West Virginia, Danny met a lovely lady sailor, Vikki. She was by his side during Dan's funeral and thereafter to hold his hand. Their romance flourished, and I had a new person to worry about—sheesh! During the winter of 2006–2007, Vikki was deployed to Iraq while Danny went to Diego Garcia. That was my first Christmas without all the kids. It could have been an exceedingly sad Christmas. However, my military mom poem had enough verses to cover anything that came with loving children in harm's way. I knew I'd survive. I sent both of them the same brain-teaser problem book to solve together via e-mail or telephone. I made a little two-minute video and put it on YouTube for them to watch. It is a horrible production, but the kids seemed to love it. They think I'm funny even when I'm not trying to be.

Last September (2007), Danny and Vikki were married in California. It was a beautiful, intimate wedding on the beach. The happy couple looked so cute dressed in traditional wedding attire, but for the flip-flops on their feet. I could not have been happier and I do believe my husband, Dan, was rejoicing from his heavenly abode. Now when I call Vikki and her voice mail says, "This is Petty Officer Vikki Lynch," I always smile. She did not keep her last name; she took ours. I hope someday I can pass on to her how to learn that poem, and for God's sake, give me a grandchild!

Danny left for Iraq around the first of March. Of course, this deployment is a challenge for me. I accept that I am no longer the number-one gal in his life and rightly so. His daily calls are to his wife. I do know he is in western Iraq and frequently goes outside the wire to work. He does have a laptop and a MySpace page. It is not difficult to keep track of him. No matter where our guys and gals are in that desert—even with no hot food, air conditioning, or toilets—they've got the Internet! I'm not sure if that is a blessing or a curse. If I do not see online activity or receive e-mails, after a week I start to panic. In the last century, before laptops and wireless Internet, it took about a month of silence before my angst burglarized my brain. The good news is that friends and acquaintances are very supportive. Frequently, they will ask about Danny and Vikki. This means the world to me, since I believe every kind thought for the kids is a prayer rising through the heavens to God's ear, and a happy verse in the poem I am learning. All I have to do is see them.

His e-mails and occasional phone calls are short and to the

point. The subject line says, "Greetings from Paradise" and continues, "Just a little note to let you all know I am safe and HAVING A BLAST . . . not really. Keep us in your prayers."

A dear friend had her second-grade students write letters to Danny. He wrote back to the class thanking them for the letters and went into great detail answering the questions that only seven-year-olds would ask, and offering this simple, but true, description of his experience in Iraq: "It is just like camping, but a lot more dangerous."

When I see a young person in uniform, I go out of my way to thank them for their service. Some look touched by the kindness and others look at me like I'm the one who is touched. No matter; it makes me feel more connected to Danny. Every day my heart hurts with an unrelenting twinge. I treat it as a reminder to remember the men and women in uniform. I do believe my poetic journey has taken me to a place where I've found new questions, ones that give me peace. I no longer ask why bad things happen; I ask God to show me what He wants me to do when bad things happen. It is then I find peace.

A senior paralegal for Legal Aid, Eileen Lynch works with victims of domestic violence with the hope of improving their lives through civil legal remedies. Eileen is the mother of four children. She was widowed after thirty-two years of marriage to her high school sweetheart, Dan. In her spare time, Eileen enjoys quilting, sewing, and cooking—and the company of many wonderful friends.

Longing for Your Safe Return

Dorothy Thomas

I AWOKE STARTLED AND CONFUSED when the phone rang at 2 A.M. on a Saturday in July. My thoughts raced back to my son's first deployment in Iraq two years ago. Twice during that six-month tour in the summer and fall of 2006, David had called during the wee hours of the night sobbing hysterically over an incident that he had just been involved in. The feelings of fear, desperation, and helplessness came over me as I prayed, "Please, God, let him be okay." This time it was different—he just wanted to talk. He had just finished breakfast on base in Iraq and was leaving for a mission in a few hours with his unit. As the conversation continued for a half hour, it became clear that he didn't want to hang up—he wanted to touch home, to hear loved ones' voices (to connect with some sense of sanity and normalcy).

David, born Sang Chul Kee on December 18, 1985, is the younger of our two sons. Shortly after adopting our older son, my husband, Brad, and I decided to begin the adoption process for a second child. About two and a half years later, David, who was eighteen months old, arrived from Korea. Not having gone through a foreign adoption before, Brad and I found things like food, language, and sleeping arrangements to be challenging transitions for all of us. Throughout school, David's natural artistic abilities, which were apparent by the time he was a preschooler, blossomed. His outgoing and very social nature makes him a happy person and fun to be around. He has always cared deeply about the people he becomes close to. Knowing how very sensitive David is about the well-being of others, Brad and I were very surprised and concerned about his decision to enlist in the U.S. Army.

After having enlisted in the Army for three years and sixteen weeks, David began fourteen weeks of basic training at Fort Leonard Wood, Missouri, on January 20, 2006. Subsequently, he settled in for his advanced training as an engineer at Fort Hood, Texas, and then was deployed to Iraq in June. During his first week in Iraq, we received a call from him at about 2 A.M. one night. He had been shot at during night patrol, but, thank God, his protective vest took the bullet, not his chest. What made him so hysterical was the fact that he returned the fire and shot an Iraqi. David was involved in or witnessed many more horrible situations during that six-month deployment. His unit returned home in November of that year. When David came home for two weeks that Christmas, we saw and heard how his experience in Iraq had scarred him mentally and emotionally. We suggested that he talk to a chaplain and seek counseling.

From the time of his return from the first deployment to the time of his second deployment, David had been stationed at Fort Hood, during which time he had received additional training. He is currently a Specialist 4 and was redeployed for his second tour in June 2008. Before leaving for Iraq, David told us that he would be protecting supplies on convoys, and that he would be a machine gunner on a Humvee. Talking to him recently, we learned that he is on a mission to construct an outpost in southern Iraq. He and his unit are away from the base for three weeks at a time.

Although David is good about contacting us as soon as he gets back to base, communication does not occur as frequently as we would like. David prefers phoning so that he can hear our voices, and he is always concerned about us worrying and wanting us to know that he is safe.

In some ways my life's journey while David is deployed seems so disconnected. So many times I find myself going into a numb zone. I can't think about where he is. It seems surreal—like he's really not there, in harm's way. It's too big to get my thoughts and emotions around—too much to comprehend. I find myself unable at times to focus on his rank, his job in the Army, or his location. Even after it has been explained to me, sometimes I just can't hold on to it. Yet on another level, I understand exactly where he is and what his job is, and the need to stay connected to my son—so there are the mailed packages, the letters and e-mails of encouragement and love. I would have much more difficulty getting through his deployment if I did not have my faith, family, and friends. Trusting deeply that God is in the midst of whatever happens, I experience much hope and strength. Knowing that family is there (especially my husband), walking the journey with me and supporting me, gives me much comfort. Friends deeply touch me when they ask about David and add that he is in their prayers. There is nothing more powerful. Besides faith, family, and friends, I have found that keeping busy and having a positive outlook rooted in my faith helps me to cope. Around the time of David's enlistment, I enrolled in a graduate-level course at St. Mary's Seminary and Graduate School of Theology and was also accepted into the Pastoral Ministry program in the Diocese of Cleveland. Between class work and my job, I am busy and enjoying both.

My experience as a mother of a soldier has given me a greater appreciation not only for those serving in the military, but also for the sacrifices and struggles their families endure. It has also helped me to see the human side of the Iraqi people through the eyes of my son.

In closing, I would like to share part of a conversation I had with David after an awards ceremony at Fort Hood, and also part of a letter he sent to us during his second deployment.

A year after returning from his first tour in Iraq, David had three weeks of desert training in California. The first weekend back at Fort Hood after this training, David was hoping to just relax. But, later that Friday afternoon, my husband and I each found ourselves on the phone with our son, trying to calm and reassure him that he would be okay.

Earlier that day, he and his unit had participated in an awards ceremony at which he received a Purple Heart for being injured in Iraq. He was then to receive the prestigious Army Commendation Medal for combat service. The way he interpreted this experience, or what he thought he heard his captain say, was "This medal is for the Iraqis you killed." As the captain started to pin on David's medal, my son "snapped," and said he could not accept the medal. "What's the difference between an American, an Iraqi, and an insurgent? It's life. How can we do this?"

His interpretation of his captain's response was that it was no big deal, and that my son should just accept the medal. David ended up walking out and calling us from his room. As I listened to him, my heart was breaking. He couldn't understand how he could get an award for killing people. "It's like pinning sin on me. It just doesn't make sense. You don't get a medal for taking a life." He couldn't understand how his twenty-four-year-old captain could joke about combat and glorify it as if it were a fairy tale. In his eyes, those who have experienced combat and have done the "grunt work" know the reality.

David started to relive events as he explained how he witnessed two friends get killed—one gunned down and one blown up. He second-guessed himself by wondering if he could have pulled them down or could have scanned the area better. As he explained to me how he felt "dirty inside," and that his "spirituality was ruined," I felt tears flowing from my eyes. How do we heal him and all those who have been affected by war? Do I expect my prayers to be answered the way I would like, or do I trust that no matter what happens, God is always in control and in the midst of my life (and David's)?

Both my husband and I believe that David suffers from post-traumatic stress disorder (PTSD). David has admitted that he feels "all messed up, dirty inside," like he "is vomiting inside." He has difficulty sleeping, even with sleep aids, and has recurring nightmares. He has used alcohol to self-medicate and is easily agitated, which is so foreign to David's personality. I had been encouraging him to seek professional help, and he finally saw an Army psychiatrist for a few sessions. Will David be able to see that God's healing can be mediated through the person who is giving him the professional help he needs? Will he believe that it is possible to be forgiven, if that is what he is seeking, and maybe more importantly, will David be able to forgive himself? My husband and I will continue to pray for, encourage, and help David in whatever way we can as we learn more about PTSD. I thank God for people like Sergeant Rod, who took David to the clinic, and for all those who help in any way with the healing process of our service men and women.

The following was written by David in a letter we recently received, a month after he arrived in Iraq for his second tour:

> Being back here scares me. I remember Granado's last deployment—dead in the body bag. I remember seeing the children and their mangled bodies, their proof of the war their torn limbs and parentless households. I smell the bodies burning and the women crying, the waters turning red with blood, all that shit from last deployment re-surfacing! I

am now living my nightmares which have haunted me! I can't hold strong to faith in a land even God forsakes. If there's God here, I have yet to see Him. My fear is to come back a different person, one you won't call your son. I fear I will become what I fear: death. It turns my heart black being here. So much death and hate and brutality! This is the place Dante describes: "the inferno fueled by hate and wanton disregard for life. The place so hot the inhabitants sweat tears of blood; where angels fall forever into a pit of fire."

We pray for the safe return of our nation's sons and daughters so that the healing may begin.

Dorothy Thomas taught in public schools for twelve years before adopting her two sons. She enjoys working in the garden, cooking, hiking, and sewing when time allows. Currently, she takes much pride and satisfaction in ministering at Holy Martyrs Catholic Church.

My Heart and Hank

Mary

As a mom of a soldier, I can honestly say that my heart changed when my son, Michael, received his first set of orders for deployment. I can remember when my cousin was killed in the Vietnam War. Those war images flashed before me. I thought to myself, "This can't happen to him; he's in the reserves." My heart became, for lack of a better term, swollen.

After 9/11, Michael was in his senior year of college. He was so emotionally distracted by the attacks, he no longer could focus on the material at hand. Using all his charm, he convinced me that he wanted to prepare himself to help preserve our country's future, whatever events might come.

He approached the private university he attended and asked if he could leave mid-term to join the reserves. He wanted to go to boot camp as an enlisted soldier and return later to finish school. One month later, Michael enlisted for six years "for all the right reasons," as he put it. Michael explained that he would be more respected by his fellow soldiers in the future if he joined the enlisted side of the branch first, before becoming an officer.

The president of the university was very supportive, but also requested that Michael promise to return and finish school when he got back from boot camp. He gave Michael great advice. He told Michael that they would reimburse his first-semester tuition if Michael promised to come back and finish the classes he needed for his bachelor's degree. After a smile and a firm handshake, it was a deal.

When Michael returned from a grueling boot camp, his sister and I were relieved. The swelling of my heart was subsiding. We just couldn't envision training so rigorously—sit-ups, push-ups, running, and the infamous gas chamber. He did it all without complaining. So many had quit! Michael's integrity wouldn't allow him to give up. That's just Michael. We flew in to attend his ceremony and couldn't have been prouder. There were lots of happy tears.

Because Michael believes that "a handshake is as important as your word," he immediately returned to the university and finished his senior year. I remember thinking, "He has a college degree and is a United States soldier!"

It was a proud moment to see my father, a World War II veteran, and the grown daughter of my cousin who was killed in the Vietnam War onstage at the ceremony pinning Michael when he became a second lieutenant at officers' school.

In the reserves, Michael now had to serve one weekend a month and two weeks a year. Focusing on his civilian career, Michael was hired by a Fortune 500 company. The company fully understood his commitment to the military and emphasized to him that they fully supported all of our armed forces. Michael did extremely well in corporate America. However, that soon came to a halt when he received orders for his first deployment.

During one of his training weeks, Michael was filmed in action learning the required skills. How was it possible for my son to appear in a training film at such a young age? My heart was bursting with pride and anxiety all at once. I kept watching it over and over. I kept looking at his thumb, his hands, his fingers, his face, and his smile. I thought to myself, "Where did the time go?" I still recall those little fingers and that thumb holding his baby bottle. I stared and stared at the clips of him. I hadn't seen him in a while. This was the next best thing. I thanked God and prayed for the person who filmed my son. I didn't know who he was, but he truly helped heal my heart that day.

As the months passed I tried my best to take care of my heart. I stopped watching the news. I put together care packages, but my most important job was caring for Michael's purebred golden retriever puppy, Hank. I recall Michael telling me that the last time he drove away to leave Hank, he looked back at him, knowing Hank would be so much bigger and older the next time he saw him. Michael told me privately that it broke his heart. There's that word again. Maybe the emotions I instilled in Michael throughout his childhood run as deep as mine. Or, maybe he simply absorbed them through our deep family ties while he was growing up. Either way, I'll take the credit for his loving nature and unwavering loyalty.

I think that Michael's unconditional love for family, country, and his dog is mirrored in Hank. That may sound humorous, but there are similarities. When Michael was in grade school, each year the teachers would say something like this on his report card: "Every day Michael comes into the classroom with a big smile." It amazed me because Michael attended four elementary schools due to career changes within our family. Today Michael still smiles from ear to ear as soon as he walks into a room—he's so very happy to see you. Just like Hank!

Still, taking care of Hank with a smile on my face has been a process. I never saw myself caring for a dog that I never asked for or even wanted. For the love of Michael, I am. Michael knew I was more than hesitant about animals and completely clueless on their needs. I would tell Michael when he was little, "Animals belong in a zoo, and if you ever want to see them, I will take you there any time!" But with the help of friends, family, and a great vet, Hank is thriving! He waits for the day when Michael will walk back through the door. The last time Michael was home on leave, Hank ran up to him and licked him frantically and never left his side. It was obvious there was a bond between them that would never change. No orders, deployments, distance, or even the enemy can ever change the fact that Hank sits and waits until his master comes home.

Michael had months of special training and many hours of school by this point. Deployment was inevitable! We kept in contact through e-mail and phone calls, but conversations were limited due to the nature of the mission.

One Sunday, I was sitting in church and looked behind me only to see a young mom holding a baby boy with a baby military suit identical to one that Michael had received as a gift when he was born. I was feeling a little emotional that day. I quickly got up, went to the back of the church, and informed the young mother that my son had the same outfit. She graciously smiled and asked me where my son was. I said he was on a deployment. She softly grabbed my hand and said, "I'll keep you and your son in my prayers." I thanked her and returned to my seat. My heart was missing Michael.

As I watch the calendar year, I notice that Michael will still be in the Middle East on his birthday. That just happens to be Mother's Day, too! I did the usual packing for his birthday present. Ideas for care packages are getting harder and harder. So, I keep it simple. He in turn sent my Mother's Day present. A few more gifts were to follow. Michael is very generous and sends gifts to all of our family members. I would be remiss if I didn't mention that I truly appreciate the cards and gifts sent to Michael over these deployments by our good friends and family. It is an indescribable feeling to know that they take the time in their busy lives to show Michael that they care.

Due to the nature of Michael's mission, being discreet is of utmost importance. Phone calls are mostly one-sided, and I have learned that he would rather hear about what is happening here at home. No worries though! Hearing his voice is enough for my pulse to slow down and keep that blood flowing steadily to my heart.

I am very strong at times when I rely on my faith, as I should daily. When worldly distractions consume and overwhelm me, my outlook can change quickly. I will always remain grateful to God for keeping Michael safe. I refuse to be self-centered about Michael's choice to be in the military. I would rather focus on his great accomplishments and how he has managed to inspire others, young and old.

My son doesn't know I wrote this essay. You will not see his last name, but what you must know is that my son, Michael, will always be there to protect you and your freedoms.

Today, Michael is in the Middle East and has recently been promoted to captain. My heart is somewhat sore, but not swollen like in the past. I attribute that to Michael. He told me once that if I'm okay, he's okay. I never knew that! He told me he could concentrate and stay focused on his mission much easier knowing that his mom, dad, little sister, and grandparents are okay. I make that my mission. When we hear from Michael by e-mail or phone from the Middle East, I make sure that he knows all is well at home. It is—except for my heart, until he comes home. That will be our little secret.

Hey, Ma!

Bernadette Swancer

MY SON, ANDREW (WE call him Andy), joined the Air Force in April of 2001. As my husband and I dropped him off at the recruiter's office, we exchanged our hugs and a few tears. I said that I wasn't going to cry, and I held up pretty well until we started to leave and Andy hollered down the hall, "Hey, Ma! Don't forget I love you!" Soon Andy was on his way to Malmstrom Air Force Base in Great Falls, Montana.

On September 11, 2001, I was watching *Good Morning America* with a friend. As we witnessed the second plane hit the twin towers, I had to call Andy! My knees were so weak that she had to hand me the phone. My reassurance that Andy was okay finally came at 1 P.M., when I heard his voice: "Hey, Ma! I love you."

In May of 2002, Andy called to say he was headed for Iraq. My heart sank. When he jokingly said, "Don't worry about me unless they bring me home in a body bag!" I really lost it. We finally had to say our goodbyes and hang up. I prayed a lot and watched the news, but watching made it worse for me, so I just prayed. In fact, when Andy entered the service, we made a pact. I said, "When you get to feeling down, say a Hail Mary." And every day, at exactly three o'clock in the afternoon, I would say, "I love you, Andy." This is what got me through.

Andy was able to make it home just in time for his wedding on May 10, 2003. He stood so proud and looked so handsome waiting for Laura to walk up the aisle. I was brimming with pride and joy as I watched my son get married. Soon they were transferred to Spangdahlem Air Force Base in Germany.

It was a year since I had last seen Andy and Laura when the phone rang, and once again, Andy was headed for Iraq. And once again, I could not even hug him goodbye. At least I would be seeing Laura over the holidays.

During the Thanksgiving holiday of 2004, I fell and broke my hip. No one was to tell Andy—I felt he had enough to worry about.

That December, I lay in the hospital with my hip pinned and screwed together. From there, I went to a nursing home to learn how to walk again. Andy was always on my mind. On Christmas Day I was feeling sorry for myself, and I wondered what kind of a Christmas he would be having in Iraq. Then, the nurse came into my room with a phone. I asked who it was, and she just answered, "Some guy." "Hello," I said, and all I heard was "Hey, Ma! I love you! Merry Christmas!" Tears flowed hard and fast. God had answered my prayers. Andy had to get special permission from his sergeant for that call. It was a Christmas I will never forget, and to this day I cannot tell the story or write about it without tears flowing. At home, my husband, Dave, received the following Christmas e-mail.

Sent: Saturday, December 25, 2004 3:14 AM
Subject: Read at the Swancer family gathering

Dear Everybody,
Thank you for the cards, gifts and goodies. Grandma, the guys

are wild about the blonde brownies. I am doing very well here in deep south Iraq. I am so close to Kuwait that I can almost spit across the border. Any how, I am working in the military equivalent of The Department of Public Works. I am planning various projects from dealing with personnel build up to the ongoing detention of insurgents, don't worry I do not work any where near the prisoners. I do occasionally have to go down into the prison to monitor various contracted projects. I do wish I could be there for the annual playing of carols and magoo. I have Charlie Brown's Christmas down here with me so it's not a total loss. It's really sad to see the level of poverty down here. This area used to be a lush green area, until Saddam dammed up the waterways and dried it up. Whenever I went on convoys, all the little children would run to the edge of the road jumping and cheering as we drove by. We would toss little goodie bags to them even though we weren't supposed to. We are still providing a lot of humanitarian relief to them. As I said before, this is a severely poverty-stricken area. These people got hit hard during the first Gulf War. As Iraq mowed them over when they invaded Kuwait, we mowed the Iraqis back over the same area, so needless to say there are a lot of bombed out homes and structures. I have also met a lot of nice Iraqis as well. There is a contractor whom I work with named Mohammed. Everyday he tells me in broken English, "America is so good, we used to be so poor, now we have freedom again." So my view on Muslims is that they are just like us, there are great people here, but then there are "bad apples." When I saw my first Iraqi, I was skeptical, but then I got to know him and he is as nice as any American. Well, I will close for now.

Mah a ssalaama (farewell in Arabic)
Andy

We thanked God when Andy returned safe and sound from this deployment, but then in May of 2006—you guessed it—the phone rang again, and Andy was headed back to Iraq for the third time! But this time was different, as he was in Afghanistan for seven months. I really needed something to do, so I joined a few military moms at my church who were packing boxes for our troops. Andy had called from Afghanistan and asked if we could send some missalettes from our church. The troops were visited by a priest or minister about once every six weeks. Since Lent was coming up, Andy, a chaplain's assistant, could hold a prayer service once a week. So, my friend Carol and I went up to church and asked the janitor where the missalettes were kept. I told him we needed them for a prayer service—I just never mentioned where the prayer service was going to be! We boxed them up and shipped them off that day! I felt God wouldn't mind helping the guys who didn't have anything. Besides the "contraband missalettes," we also sent rosary beads, prayer books, and religious reading material for Chaplain Fulton, Andy's chaplain, to hand out.

We military moms really connected as we laughed and cried together. Our sons belonged to all of us. On August 4, 2006, I heard that soldiers from our Brook Park, Ohio, Marines unit were killed. One of our moms, Mary Anne, had a son from that unit. I immediately called our church to see if her son was among them. Whew! Thank God! He wasn't killed. The following October, I was watching the news on the day her son was supposed to land in the United States and saw a bedsheet with the words "Welcome Home Stan" on it. I grabbed the phone, excited to tell Mary Anne that Stan was home safe! She and her husband watched for that sheet all evening on the news! This is the kind of support we gave to one another.

November 2006, and no news from Andy as all hell was breaking loose over there. Finally he called to say he was safe. Laura and I were in constant contact. We e-mailed every day, and sometimes twice a day.

By this time we had worn out our welcome at the local post office. The postal clerk, George, had grown rather grumpy. So I showed up early, like I always did, and there was an elderly lady in front of me. "Oh no! We have George today!" I exclaimed. She said, "What's wrong with him?" I said that he was very grumpy, and then I told her why. "It's because he suffers from hemorrhoids." I had no idea she was going to repeat this! So she gets up to the counter and George was his grumpy old self, and she says to him, "I understand your problem. I, too, suffer from hemorrhoids. I know the pain you are in!" I wanted to die of embarrassment. There were quite a few of us in line. Needless to say, I started going to another post office!

It has been five years since I have seen Andy. He hopes to come home in August of 2008. He will be transferred to Spokane, Washington, in November of 2008. God, what I wouldn't give to put my arms around him and finally give him a hug! I always hug my three other boys, but how much I have missed hugging Andy! What I wouldn't give to hear "Hey, Ma!" in person! It's a mother's special love for her children. We love them more than they will ever know.

Bernadette Swancer and her husband, Dave, have four boys and enjoy being grandparents. Bernadette loves to spend time in her kitchen, especially devising new recipes. She once entered a cooking contest with a recipe she had never tried before—and won. She is a tireless worker when it comes to supporting all of our soldiers.

Team Fawley

Annie Fawley

THE COUNTDOWN HAD BEGUN. I now had a date when my son would be leaving for Iraq. Fear, apprehension, and concern consumed my being. I played out every possible horrible scenario in my mind, because now I was faced with the possibility of losing my beloved son. The time moved so quickly. He was home for leave. Did I do enough for him—make all his favorite foods, go all the places he wanted to go, listen to his every word?

We were down to the last few days before he left. I helped clean and pack his first apartment, took him to his favorite restaurants, bought him an iPod, and held back the tears. The moment came. I held him tight so I would never forget how he felt. I touched his face so I would never forget how handsome he is. I tried to fill my being with his smell so I would always have him with me. With tears flowing down my cheeks, I sent my son to war.

The countdown to his coming home was on. I poured myself into writing letters, sending the comics, searching out articles he would find interesting, and mailing packages. I put on a brave face when people asked how he was and how I could handle it. I told them he was doing the job he wanted, he was well trained, and he seemed to be all right. What I really wanted to say was: I worry about him every moment of every day. I wake in the middle of the night panicked, thinking about how he's in a remote area. I ask questions that cannot possibly be answered: Are they on patrol? Is there an IED (improvised explosive device) under their vehicle? Are shots being fired? My soldier tells me not to worry—"They're not very good shots." It is mildly reassuring. I watch the news and hold my breath. Is my son the one who was killed? Will I turn the corner on the way home from work and see a car with soldiers in uniform outside my house? I go to his room, smell his sheets, run my fingers over his mementos. I miss him so much.

I am more concerned with his welfare than my own. When people in line at the bank complain about the heat I want to say, "This is nothing compared to what my son is living in." When I see guys he went to high school with I want to grab them by the neck and scream, "Why aren't you over there?" My relationships are strained. I need to do something.

And then I started to run, miles and miles, working out my stress and anger. It became a connection with my son; he became part trainer, part nutritionist, and big-time enthusiast. I kept him up to date on my mileage, described my running club partners, debated whether I should train for a marathon. He was my biggest supporter, saying, "Go for it, Mom!" A week before he was scheduled to be home, I did run that marathon with him as my inspiration. We're tough; we don't quit. If he could handle a year at war, I could run 26.2 miles.

We drove his car back to Fort Drum and anxiously tried to pick him out at the welcome-home ceremony. There was so much excitement and pride in that auditorium. All of a sudden a huge hug caught me by surprise. Sobbing, I clung to him, and with his words—"It's okay, Mom, I'm home, it's over"—I crossed back to normal.

This is my epilogue: When he was home, he went to my running club with me and met everyone, and ran with us. He was an instant hit. The idea was planted—we would run a marathon together. Team Fawley was born. So on a cool day in May, we ran that marathon. He met me at the finish line with shirts printed "Team Fawley—Like Mother, Like Son."

Annie Fawley works as a paralegal and is active in her church. She and her husband, Darrell, have two children. Annie recently took up running seriously and has completed three marathons. She plans to do the Ford Ironman in Florida with her son, Captain Darrell E. Fawley III.

Two Voices of War

Mary Long

IT WAS MOTHER'S DAY, 2006—my first without my son, Jeff. A Marine, Jeff had been stationed at Camp Baharia in Fallujah, Iraq, from January to October of 2006. He was a gunner on a security team for a motor transportation unit. It was his first deployment—one too many as far as I was concerned! In a family of five daughters, he is my only son. Jeff's team provided support, supplies, and security on convoys, patrols, resupply runs, wrecker runs, and any other missions that they were told to complete. We knew the inherent danger he was in, and the days since his departure had been long and agonizing, as we never knew what to expect. Each day was focused on his life "over there," and it was torment trying to fall asleep each night.

> It's a whole other world over here. It's hot, it's dry, it's dangerous . . . it's depressing. Our days are long, and our nights are sometimes longer. I quickly learned to trust only the men wearing the same uniform as me. As for the Iraqi civilians compared to the insurgents, you cannot tell who is who, unless one is shooting at you and the other is not. Even then, you still never know.

There were tears, fears, and insecurity, and I felt like I was unable to cope. I was always wondering what Jeff was doing, how he was feeling and coping, when we would hear from him, or if my ultimate fear—Marines at our door, informing us of the worst—would become a reality.

> Being on the road in one of the world's most dangerous cities every day and every night you see a lot of crazy things. I have experienced everything from IEDs, fire fights, RPG fire, and grenades being thrown at us, to Iraqi kids waving their hands and smiling as I tossed candy and water out of the turret of my Humvee. Like I said, it's crazy over here.

Only a mother who carried her child till birth, and cried at the joy of the first sound of that baby, can truly understand how agonizing this time was. Knowing Jeff was in harm's way, I lived in prayer day and night.

> You are just driving along the same roads like you do everyday, and then all of a sudden—BOOM! An IED goes off, and then it's silent, or at least it seems to be for a few minutes, but it really isn't. I'll never forget the first time we got hit, or the first time I had to fire my rifle . . . I can't explain it. War is something that is extraordinary, devastating, great, depressing, happy, sad, and every other emotion a human can feel mixed somewhere in between the rest of them. I can't put it into words . . . Unless you have lived it personally, you will never understand.

If it was not for the support of my husband, daughters, family, and friends, I could not have made it through. I love them all, each individually for the blessing they are. On this Mother's Day,

Jeff's absence was profoundly felt by all of us. It had been one long month since we last heard from him. All sorts of memories floated in my head of Jeff as a little boy, and now of Jeff, the man, serving our country. I was frightened to think that this could be my last Mother's Day with all of my children. And yet, how proud I was! My heart was overflowing as I thought of his courage and integrity. Jeff loves his country. He will fight for our freedom and safety, no matter the cost.

> Being in Iraq makes me realize how lucky we are to be American. It also makes me realize how many people take it for granted. We did not become the country we are by getting everything handed to us. We had to fight for it! A lot of people don't realize what we have to go through so you can live in a free country. I could go on and on, but I won't. Just remember, if you come across anyone who has served or is serving, make sure to thank them for what they have done or what they are doing.

Our family had gone to Holy Martyrs Church together and returned home for a Mother's Day breakfast. My husband began to pray before we ate our meal. Just at the moment when he asked our Lord to keep Jeff safe, the phone rang. It was Jeff! In my heart, I knew a miracle had just happened! It was, and always will be, the best Mother's Day gift ever. We all had a chance to talk with him. Then we all gave thanks.

Jeff returned home safely in October of 2006. He is still a Marine reservist with two more years of duty. I continue to pray daily for every mother who has agonized through the experience of sending her son or daughter to war. I especially pray for every mother whose soldier has made the ultimate sacrifice. For there, but for the grace of God, go I.

I consider myself very lucky in many ways. Lucky that I came home to my family and friends alive and not injured. Lucky that I had the opportunity to serve my country in a time of war. Lucky that God gave me the ability to be a United States Marine. Lucky to have the tremendous support of family and friends. Lucky to have served with some of the country's finest and bravest men. Lucky to have experienced something that most Americans never will.

Mary Long is a nurse and the mother of six children, and grandmother of eight. She prays daily for the families whose lives have been affected by war.

Ten Years from Now

Anonymous

"TEN YEARS FROM NOW, I'll be in some third world country taking out terrorists. Why? Because I'll be an officer in command of a U.S. Navy SEAL team, working with the best of the best."

These are the words my son wrote in his senior year of high school. They appear in his yearbook on a page entitled "Glimpse into the Future." While most of the comments on this page are quite entertaining and quite unbelievable, this particular one is different. My son missed his ten-year class reunion. Why? Because he was in Iraq as a member of a U.S. Navy SEAL team, working with the best of the best.

To be a U.S. Navy SEAL had been my son's dream since he was in junior high. Most everything he did was done with the specific intent of helping him to achieve that goal. A SEAL flag hung on his bedroom wall as a constant reminder that some day he would be a SEAL. The tattered black SEAL T-shirt that he always wore served as a reminder to him and me of his dream for the future. While his younger brother lay in bed, assigned the job of counting, my son did hundreds of sit-ups. As he wore a path in the snow to the willow tree in our backyard to do his pull-ups, his double chin and chubby physique disappeared. He did it all for his dream—his dream of being a Navy SEAL.

He enrolled in college, participated in ROTC, and struggled to earn an engineering degree. The focus on his dream continued as he strengthened his skills. As a member of the sailing and water polo teams, he developed a comfort in the water that would later prove to be beneficial. He learned to scuba dive and continued his rigorous exercise routine. Finally, after five years of college, he graduated and enlisted in the Navy with a guarantee that he would have the opportunity to at least try out for the SEALs.

I will never forget the day that we drove him to meet the SEAL motivator and say goodbye as they shipped him off to boot camp. Along the way, I remember his father asking him an interesting question.

"If they weren't going to pay you to do this, would you still do it?"

He replied, "It depends on how much it would cost me."

That was the dedication this young man possessed. How could a mother be selfish and try to discourage her son from achieving his dream? It was not my dream for him, but that was not what was important. It was his dream.

My son graduated from boot camp as the honor recruit, and then came his opportunity to go through BUD/S (Basic Underwater Demolition/SEAL) training. You may have seen the TV shows about this experience. His uncle bought him the entire series years before, so we thought we had an idea of what he would be going through. Over the next several months, he would call when he could and give us reports on how many more had rung the bell and made the decision to drop out. The fastest had quit. The strongest had quit. Some of the officers had quit. We could only pray that he would be safe and have the strength to never quit, because this was the dream he had worked so hard for.

Hell Week was the finale and worse than anyone could imagine. Finally, we got the call. He had made it! That was only the beginning. There were several more months of training and testing before he finally qualified to become part of a SEAL team. We flew out to California to attend his graduation, which only contained 22 of the original 168 classmates. While we had attended his school graduations before, this one had an entirely different meaning.

Months of specialized training followed. It was great to know that he was in the States, even though he was doing extremely dangerous things. As a SEAL, he trained for sea, air, and land missions and was participating daily in activities that most people would never do in their entire lives. He lived his life like all SEALs do, knowing that "the only easy day was yesterday." This was his dream.

The time finally arrived when he had to use this training and was scheduled for deployment. Once again, we went out to California to spend some time with him. He was anxious and ready to go. I will never forget the strength of that last hug goodbye.

Thank goodness for e-mail. I cannot imagine what it must have been like during other wars, when loved ones would wait for weeks and months to hear from soldiers. Every day I eagerly checked my e-mail and awaited his messages. Even one word would assure me that he was safe—at least for that moment. Regularly, I would send him e-mails from home in the hope that he would know he was always in our thoughts. "Stay safe. Love ya lots."

Coming out of church one day, I met the mother of a wounded soldier who said to me, "These guys have no idea what they are doing for their mothers' prayer lives."

I clung to that realization. This was his dream, and there was nothing that I could do to protect him now except pray. So, pray I did. Every day that he was deployed, I prayed a rosary and put his care completely in God's hands. It was all that I could do. It was the least that I could do. Not once did I go to sleep without praying that rosary for my son and the others at war with him.

Care packages were sent on a regular basis, as I tried to think of something that he could use or enjoy, something that would brighten his day as he battled in the summer heat of Iraq's desert. He had very few requests, so when one did come along, I was excited to be able to comply. One time, to my pleasant surprise, I was actually able to find the exact style and size of running shoes that he requested. Or so I thought. When he finally received the shoes weeks later, he graciously thanked me for them, but mentioned one little problem. The last time he checked he only had one left foot, and I had sent him two left shoes! He said he also checked around to see if any of the other guys had two left feet and could use them, but no one did. Once again, I realized that the best thing that I could do for him was pray.

Soon my son would be "celebrating" his birthday in Iraq. I wanted desperately to help make that day special for him. The "Birthday Card Campaign for a Soldier" was born. What started out as an e-mail request to some of our friends and relatives to send him a birthday card led to bags of birthday cards that kept coming for over a month.

One advantage to being in the Special Forces was that he had access to special equipment, and he was able to call home often. In fact, despite the fact that he was in a very different time zone, he called on every family member's actual birthday. It was amazing that despite what he was enduring, he remembered all of our special days!

Telephone conversations were rather one-sided. My son could not tell us what he was doing. At times, he could not tell us where he was. We quickly learned that we had to be careful about the questions we asked him. It was better to just tell him what was happening back home no matter how unimportant it seemed to us. Hearing his voice was so precious that it was always so hard to hang up.

I do not read war stories or watch war movies because I cannot bear to think of those horrors. I am very selective in the television coverage that I watch. I choose to focus on the outstanding achievements of my son and the inspiration that he is to me. I choose to rely on my faith in God and my trust in Him. I pray that

God will bless my son and keep him safe. I pray that my son will find strength in God. It's the best thing I can do for him. I am ever so grateful to God that our son has now returned safely from two deployments, but there are more to come.

It would be selfish of me to wish another path for him. Why? Because I am the mother of a U.S. Navy SEAL, and he is living his dream with the best of the best.

We were recently with him at a public event where members of the military were asked to stand and be recognized for their service. Our son simply sat quietly and applauded the others. That is the way of a SEAL. You will rarely read about the medals and awards that SEALs receive, and there will be no articles in the newspaper about their deployment or return home. You won't see them in uniform at an airport. You may never know when one is in your midst.

My son has asked that I not use his name, or mine, in this story. You will not see our picture. Instead, he told me that I should create a pen name for myself. In his honor, there is really only one way that I can sign this story because I love him more than he will ever know . . .

— The Proud Mother of a Navy SEAL

The Dreaded Place

Debi Gebler

I WAS TWENTY-FOUR YEARS OLD, standing in the office of the high school I had attended and now worked at as a secretary and aide. I remember that two handsome men in military uniforms entered the office and asked for Mr. Reigel, the principal of the elementary school in the building next door. I looked over and saw that Mrs. Wyville, a long-time secretary in the building, had started to cry. I so vividly remember thinking, "Why are these men here? What do they want with Principal Reigel? And why is Mrs. Wyville crying?" I later learned that Mr. Reigel's son, First Lieutenant David Reigel, a United States Marine pilot, was killed in a jet crash on a training mission in California earlier that day. The young, handsome military men were there to inform Principal Reigel of the news.

I had not thought about that event for many years—until my second-born son, Brett Joseph Gebler, announced he wanted to join the military. I was proud and I was scared. A year and a half later, my son was on his way to Korea as an avionics electrician. I don't know what his motivation was to join. Possibly, it was the grandfather he never met, William Joseph Gebler, who served in the Korean War, or the fact that 9/11 took place during his senior year in high school and patriotism was running high. Maybe he just wasn't sure what path to take, and thought the military would give him time to sort things out and find his way.

As all recruits do, Brett took the aptitude test. He qualified to work on the electronics components (dashboards, headsets, and detection equipment) aboard helicopters. He originally wanted to pilot the helicopters, but his impaired (less than twenty-twenty) vision kept him from pursuing that, and I have to say, I was relieved. I thought it sounded "cool" and safe. I was very comfortable with it—ride in them, fix them, but don't pilot them. Perfect!

By the time he was finished with his military occupational specialty (MOS) schooling in avionics, the United States had invaded Iraq. Yikes! I didn't see that one coming a year and a half earlier when the whole military issue came up. I was relieved to find out he was going to Korea instead of Iraq. His first phone call home was made from Seoul, South Korea, a long way and a big change from Chagrin Falls, Ohio! He was amazed at the differences in culture and the size and activity of that huge city. I was just glad nobody would be firing at him. Looking back, it was the calmest of the overseas tours. I do remember the day he called in the spring of 2004 (he called quite often that year), and I knew I had to take the opportunity to tell him I had been diagnosed with breast cancer. It was hard enough on my two sons here, so I could only imagine how difficult it was to hear the news half a world away. He, of course, wanted to know everything. I'm sure he had to feel as though all was not being revealed to him regarding my condition. He e-mailed his brothers to get the "real scoop" and to check and see if I was "up and around." He quickly got his hands on a pink breast cancer rubber bracelet and wears it to this day.

The Korean year was Brett's first Christmas away from home. I knew he was desperately homesick, knowing we were all together without him. One of the networks filmed him sitting in front of a fire to tape his holiday wishes to the folks back home. We were told ahead of time when to tune in to see it on our local station. I recorded it and must have watched it forty times that night—smiling, crying, and then smiling again. At the Christmas family gathering, we all toasted him, and the toast was immediately sent to him via the Internet. More tears from both sides of the world. Having a loved one away at the holidays is very difficult.

When Brett's one-year tour of duty in Korea was over, he was in the States for a short time before he was deployed to Iraq, the dreaded place (dreaded by me, not him). Korea seemed like Disney World now. In Iraq there would be guns and mortar fire. He was stationed at Camp Anaconda, fifty miles north of Baghdad. The camp was nicknamed "Mortar-rita-ville." They guys seemed to find this nickname funny. Not me.

The high temperatures in Iraq (up to 113 degrees at times) were brutal, and Brett has never liked the heat. We were sending packages of powered drink mixes weekly. Friends, neighbors, family, and coworkers were so kind to also send packages to Brett and his friends. I was always impressed when Brett shared his packages with soldiers who didn't receive any.

We weren't able to talk to Brett as often in Iraq as we did when he was in Korea. E-mail became our lifeline. There were times I felt like I was talking to someone in prison. We, here at home, had news to share—we could discuss current events and our opinions about them. His routine was the same day in and day out. Wake up, eat, work a twelve-hour shift, eat, relax for an hour, sleep. Do it all over again the next day. I was always torn between asking when he would call again and not wanting to add to the stress he already faced.

The majority of this log was written at 3 A.M., a habit I picked up while Brett was in Iraq. I would get up in the middle of the night and watch the national news. As I finish the end of my Iraq story, my son, at twenty-four years of age, is now in Afghanistan.

He left on December 26, 2006 (my birthday). A year ago, I couldn't have told you where it was on a map, but now I could give you the mean temperature for July.

It seemed (to the mother of a soldier, anyway) that the fighting in Afghanistan had escalated by the time he arrived. The attempt on Vice President Cheney's life by a suicide bomber occurred outside his base a week or so after he got there. I soon learned that when an "incident" such as that occurs, all communications to the outside are shut down.

I watch the news too much. Too many helicopters go down. Brett's on them all the time. I keep telling myself, "Everything will be all right; he will be just fine." Then it happens, and it happens too close to home—one of Brett's buddies from high school, a Marine, is killed in Iraq.

Cards and flowers were sent, meals were made, ceremonies and memorials were attended, and prayers were said. The Marine who died, Sergeant Michael M. Kashkoush, was not my son. Why did I feel like he was? Because he was everyone's son. The final trip Michael made down Maple Street into his beloved Chagrin Falls on a dark, cold, and blustery night in February was surely not the homecoming anyone imagined. I was sad and I was scared. I was comforted by the sensitivity of the friends who put their hand in mine or gently touched my back, understanding what I was feeling.

While he is overseas, the twelve-hour workdays and night classes have kept Brett very busy. We don't hear from him as often as we'd like. I still watch too much news, which all too often tells me a helicopter has gone down in Afghanistan or Iraq. Seven were killed and three were injured. And no word comes from my baby. And I *pray* no word comes from a couple of soldiers at my door.

As for Brett, he will be returning to the States at the beginning of this New Year, 2008. At the time of this writing, our countdown is at seven days remaining until his plane lands at Fort Bragg. And yes, I will be among the proud families and friends greeting that plane. As a mother of a soldier, I don't think I will be able to stand there without thinking of those brave families whose children will not be getting off the plane. Brett's six-year commitment to the Army will be complete in August of this year. At this time, he says he will not re-enlist. His time in Iraq and Afghanistan has been productive and relatively safe. He has grown to become a confident and caring man. The pride and love I feel for him is immeasurable.

My admiration and gratitude goes out to all the men and women who selflessly give so much, sometimes *all*, to their country. God bless all of you—*and* the loved ones who keep you in their hearts.

Debi Gebler works for her local public school system. She coached cheerleading for twenty-one years until she was diagnosed with breast cancer in 2004. She still works full time and enjoys gardening, vacationing in Quebec, and cooking. She has been married to Mark, her high school sweetheart, since 1978.

My Career as an Army Mom

Carol Sue Tengler

ON JUNE 16, 1986, a handsome eighteen-year-old boy, Edward J. Tushar Jr., left my house for the Army. I didn't know then that I would still be an Army mom twenty-two years later. I missed him terribly, but there were no major conflicts, so it was a little easier to let him go back then. He served in Korea and various bases in the States—including our Mentor, Ohio, recruiting office. He married and had children, and we saw each other often. Life was good! But each time he came home for a leave, I saw that the boy was slowly giving way to a mature, wonderful young man.

Then—Iraq happened. First Sergeant Edward J. Tushar was deployed for three tours, and is currently serving his third tour there. He also has served a tour in Kuwait. Keeping in touch throughout the three tours is paramount and top priority. He needs to know that we love him and miss him. And I need to keep in touch with him for me. There are e-mails, phone calls, funny cards, and bigger and bigger care packages leaving my house. The boxes have to be full of his favorite things. At Christmas they include Christmas trees and decorations—in the spring, Easter decorations and bunny candy. I take comfort in sending things to him and his guys and gals. Eddy set up a recreation area, so I send books, dominoes, playing cards, puzzles, and games. It makes me feel closer to him to do this for all the guys and gals under his command.

Birthdays, holidays and other special days are not the same. Eddy isn't here with us. A late-night phone call, a knock on the door, or no e-mails, and a wave of panic goes through me. He always says, "Mom, don't worry." That is so much easier said than done. I scour the Internet and newspapers for the current updates on Iraq. I look for whatever is happening with the 101st ABN DIV (airborne division)—who is hurt, what is going on, etc. This is a big mistake, but a habit that cannot be easily broken. It leads to many sleepless nights watching twenty-four-hour news stations. To ease the gnawing fear, I put yellow ribbons around our trees and an "Army Strong" sign in the front yard with red, white, and blue flowers surrounding it. I wear Army and mom pins, fly an Army flag alongside our beautiful American flag, and pray. Prayer gets you through. Without prayer and my faith, I know that I would not be as strong as I am today. Psalm 91 hangs on my refrigerator door, and it is said on every trip to the kitchen:

You who live in the shelter of the Most High,
Who abide in the shadow of the Almighty,
Will say to the Lord, "My refuge and my fortress, my God in whom I trust."
For He will deliver you from the snare of the fowler . . .
Under his wings you will find refuge;
His faithfulness is a shield . . . You will not fear the terror of the night
Or the arrow that flies by day . . .
A thousand may fall at your side . . . but it will not come near you . . .

Because you have made the Lord your refuge . . . No evil shall befall you . . .
For He will command his angels to guard you in all your ways . . .
I will protect those who know my name
When they call to me, I will answer them
I will be with them in trouble,
I will rescue them and honor them . . .

The support and prayers of family, friends, and the wonderful congregation from our church gets me through each day.

Eddy never tells me much about what is going on—he knows how much I worry—but each tour has had its own event. On one of his tours, his Humvee overturned and he was injured, but only slightly.

He runs every day at the FOB (forward operating base) with a friend. One day they decided not to run at all. Their FOB was mortared with five rounds of missiles in less than one minute. One of the rounds landed where they usually run. That same day, a soldier was killed by a mortar that went over a ten-foot concrete wall with sandbags stacked around his quarters. He died while he slept. Eddy said in his e-mail,

> I remember thinking that Someone looked out for me that day and when it's your time to go, it will happen, no matter what is protecting you.

Eddy gave me strength with those words. I am comforted knowing that our prayers have kept him safe so far, but equally comforted that he knows all is in God's hands. It is not easy to accept, but it's good to know that he feels that way. I have stood along the street too many times as a hearse goes by, carrying a fallen hero. I clutch Eddy's picture to my heart and cry for the young person and the family. I whisper a prayer for all of them, and also a prayer of thanks that Eddy is still safe. I feel like they are all my children, too. We are all connected by the camaraderie of our children in service. We are a support system, communicating by a simple wave, tear, or prayer.

With Eddy being deployed for three tours, I often worry about his mental outlook, especially now that he has men and women under his leadership. He recently told me, "I have seen the pictures of the aftermath of attacks, but it doesn't haunt me. My biggest memory is walking past the memorial wall in the Brigade TOC [tactical operations center] building at COB [Contingency Operating Base] Speicher on the last deployment and seeing those soldiers who had died during our deployment, and then standing on the memorial field at Fort Campbell as their names were revealed on the Rakkasan Memorial Wall." (Rakkasan is a nickname from the Japanese word for parachute.)

As an Army mom, I wonder if he is truly okay with it all. Time will tell. I have been an Army mom for twenty-two years. I have experienced joy, sadness, sudden panic attacks, and bouts of tears. And, believe me, even after twenty-two years, it doesn't get any easier. Every day I am proud of my soldier, as well as every other young man or woman serving our country. I am proud to be an Army mom, and proud of every other Army mom out there. Together we are strong. I still wait for e-mails, phone calls, R & R (rest and recuperation) visits, and an "I love you, Mom." And I will continue to be a proud mom after 1SG Edward J. Tushar retires. After all, no matter how old our children get, they will always be our "babies."

Carol Sue Tengler is a housewife and a mother of two sons. She and her husband, Cliff, also have ten grandchildren. In addition to her family, she enjoys her pets, her church, and life in general.

Army Strong—A Family Affair

Celeste Hicks

"DUMBFOUNDED" IS HOW I would describe my reaction when my oldest daughter, Micala, decided she wanted to attend a military academy. She pursued her dreams and chose West Point, and our military family was born. Her next four siblings chose Army ROTC rather than the academy, and our lives, already a whirlwind with seven kids, intensified. One month after 9/11, Micala was off to South Korea for a year. Protests against our army were common at the time, and one day a particularly violent crowd outside her gated post was lighting fires, shaking the fence, and screaming insults at the troops while a visiting general addressed them in formation. He told them that the Koreans were using the freedom of speech that our soldiers were there to protect! I cried . . . he was right, but it scared me.

Micala deployed to Iraq after being back in the States for about eight months. As a platoon leader (in the 87th Engineering Battalion attached to the 18th Airborne Corps) her "vertical construction" platoon helped build the base in Taqaddum (in Anbar province). Prayer and action were the only things that got me through these trying times. A friend of Micala's from West Point, Dawn, had just lost an arm to an IED, so those fears were real and ever present. Our fears were heightened when my husband received a phone call from Micala that was abruptly cut short with "Dad, I have to go . . . I hear mortar fire!" immediately followed by the phone going dead. We lived on pins and needles for a few days until finally receiving an e-mail saying she was okay.

I mailed a lot of boxes, kept all the kids in touch via e-mail, and refused to watch CNN or any other TV news. I relied instead on reading the newspaper and *U.S. News & World Report* so I could get less drama and more facts about the war . . . and I prayed incessantly. Any missed phone calls were saved on the answering machine to listen to over and over. When I heard Micala's voice I felt both relief and fear.

In the meantime, our son Nate was stationed in Germany with a transportation company. When our third child, Patrick, graduated in May of 2004, both Nate and Micala were able to be there to pin on his Second Lieutenant bars. Patrick went to Germany in January 2005, right after Nate's wedding to Kathryn Donovan in December of 2004. All of our children were in attendance. Their wedding day was the last time we have all been together under the same roof! I am desperately hoping for a reunion in December of 2008.

In December of 2005, Nate deployed to Kuwait for over a year (in command of the 260th Transportation Detachment in the 28th Transportation Battalion), while his pregnant wife stayed behind in Germany and continued to teach first grade in an international school. Charged with keeping convoys safe and vehicles working and protecting his contracted drivers, who were predominantly from nearby third world countries, Nate led a harried life. We all worried about Katie, but our prayers were answered when Nate returned to Germany for his mid-deployment R & R within three hours of his daughter's birth! I was delighted to go there a week later to see my first grandchild, but saddened to have to comfort his wife when he left to return to Kuwait a few days later. Such is life in the military.

In February of 2006, Patrick deployed to Mosul, Iraq, with the 16th Engineering Battalion, 1st Brigade Combat Team, 1st Armored Division, as a platoon leader for a combat engineering unit. After four months they moved to Ramadi, where they worked twelve-hour night shifts, rotating between scouring the roads for IEDs and blowing up insurgent strongholds or weapons caches. Patrick is my sensitive son, and I worried about his frequent headaches, his fatigue, and his near misses.

I said so many rosaries as I walked around the soccer fields while my younger children were practicing that I am sure anyone who may have been watching me thought I was crazy. I decided that I needed something to help me so that I wasn't just surviving each week, but actually living for the sake of all my kids. So I went to the doctor, was prescribed a mild anti-anxiety medicine, and was thankful that it seemed to help.

At the same time all this was going on in our lives, we were also planning a wedding for our fourth child, Mary, who had recently been commissioned a Second Lieutenant, and was stationed at Fort Sam Houston, Texas (and going to Baylor University for a master's degree in dietetics). On December 29, 2006, she married First Lieutenant Zachary Staudter, stationed at Fort Hood, Texas. Nate's company was not held over in Kuwait as feared, so he and Katie and their baby, Emma, made it home in time for the wedding. It broke Mary's heart not to have her brother Patrick there, but he was still serving in Iraq. There were definitely tears shed over his absence, as he and Mary are close, and it bothered her that he had not yet had a chance to meet his future brother-in-law. Micala was due to leave for Afghanistan in January 2007, and there were rumors that the date would be moved up, which caused a lot of stress and anguish since Micala was the maid of honor and her deployment was the reason we had the wedding in December despite Patrick's absence. Nonetheless, the wedding plans all came together and Patrick eventually made it home in March to a hero's welcome.

I was finally able to have long talks with Patrick, and I found it helpful to just sit and listen to all the things that he had had to go through. However, I broke down and cried really hard when he told me about a young private in his former platoon who was killed in a firefight on his last mission, just a few days before he was to return home from Iraq. I ached for the boy's mother, and wished I could have put my arms around her. That is why I record the death of every soldier in Operation Iraqi Freedom and Operation Enduring Freedom, and in all the training accidents associated with either one. It has become my personal prayer book for them and their families, and a memorial of sorts to the lives that have been tragically cut short.

Patrick returned to Germany to work in Heidelberg for the Deputy Chief of Staff of Engineers (ODCSENG), while Nate and Katie left active duty and moved to Ohio with nine-month-old Emma. Nate is now a captain in the reserves (in a military intelligence unit). Micala returned safely from Afghanistan in March of 2008, and I was able to welcome her back to the United States. Among many things, her battalion trained local Afghans in the construction trades and gave them each tool kits to help them establish a livelihood for their families.

In May 2008, Phillip, our fifth child, graduated from the University of Notre Dame, with Micala present to pin his Second Lieutenant bars. He is in Medical Services, preferring to have a healing role in the Army, despite graduating with a degree in mechanical engineering. He is currently on temporary duty at Fort Lewis, Washington, with Micala (as well as her boyfriend, Captain Jason Siler, who just returned from fifteen months in Baqubah,

Iraq). In October, he will attend Officer's Basic Course in Fort Sam Houston, just a week after Mary leaves to go to Fort Leonard Wood, Missouri, while her husband is at training in Fort Gordon, Georgia. They have been married a year and a half and see each other on weekends.

Patrick just left active duty at the end of June 2008 and is in a reserve unit. After all the years he was gone, I often look over at his face and realize just how blessed we are to have him back home with us. But none of this is over yet, and as Iraq seems to wind down some, Afghanistan is heating up. My rosaries will continue to get a regular workout as I pray for God to bless all our men and women in the military.

My head starts to spin when I really think about all this, and I know the only thing holding me together is my strong faith. God is always with us, and yes, there are guardian angels who protect us. I also know that my children belong to God and not really to me, and that, despite the depth of my love, His love for them is far greater.

I am incredibly proud of my amazing children! The last two, Rod and Arianna, are only fourteen and ten years old. At this moment, they say they will not serve in the Army . . . only time will tell. Until then, their older brothers and sisters will work overtime to keep us safe in the land of the free and the brave.

Celeste Hicks is a registered nurse working in coronary care. She met her husband, Michael, now a NASA engineer, in college. They wanted children to play an important role in their lives, so after having five children of their own they decided to become foster parents. They cared for ten additional children over a span of ten years. During this time they ended up adopting two children who were not able to be reunited with their birth family.

No Place Like Home

Elaina Goodrich

WHEN MY SON, MAJOR Grant Goodrich, was stationed in Austin, Texas, training Marine Corps reservists, I felt that he was relatively safe—until his unit was called up for deployment in Iraq. I worried whether a reserve unit would be less prepared for war than active-duty Marines, and therefore be in greater danger. I wondered if, as reservists, they would be placed in a safer location. As it turned out, they were very well trained and assigned to one of the most dangerous places, Anbar province, long the center of the Sunni Arab-driven insurgency against U.S. forces and their allies.

In August of 2004, Grant was deployed as an operations officer, directing units with the 1st Battalion, 23rd Marine Regiment. My husband and I focused our energies on getting him through the difficult times ahead.

During his career Grant had lived in twelve different places, but none was as unusual as his "homes" in Iraq. At Al Asad Air Base, he first lived in a large tent with eight other officers while they waited for the unit they were replacing to vacate their spaces. He thought that he would be there only two weeks, but his stay kept getting extended! Then, Grant lived in a trailer with few amenities. He asked us for rugs to get the sand off his shoes (it was everywhere!), and curtains to make it a little more like home. We included a Cleveland Browns flag, since football season was close at hand. Those items were followed with many care packages. My husband, who had served in the Army during the Vietnam War, had a box going continuously. He made weekly trips to the post office with boxes filled with local news (particularly updates on the Cleveland Indians, Browns, and Cavaliers) and snacks, especially the homemade cookies. I'm surprised that Grant didn't gain weight from all the calories, although I guess they were a hit with his unit as well. We learned that M&M's were popular, since they would miraculously survive the 110-degree-plus heat. Pringles and dried fruit were also requested frequently—it was amazing what he missed. At Christmas, the whole family sent gifts, including a small Christmas tree and wreath!

I'm certain that the ability to keep in touch with us helped Grant stay strong through his long, stressful deployment. My husband would often remind me that unless you've been through it, you cannot imagine how important it is to remember home and to have as much contact as possible. The euphoria of "mail call" can't be overemphasized.

Grant also kept in touch with his girlfriend, and she, in turn, relayed news from Iraq to us. We tried to keep tabs on where Grant was. The map of Iraq was always kept open and used as he moved from Al Asad to the Russian-built Haditha Dam, on Lake Qadisiyah along the Euphrates River. Grant was living in the actual concrete structure of this massive hydroelectric dam. This made me believe he was safer; it was certainly a substantial structure compared to a trailer or a tent! Haditha Dam was eleven stories high, without working elevators, so the Marines got plenty of exercise on the stairs. Their offices, mess hall, gym, and living areas were converted from former operations offices and hallways. Although it was built just twenty years before, much of the piping and electricity was in poor condition. The plumbing didn't work, so the Marines had to use portable toilets and showers on either the first or seventh levels. The dam was fully operational, supplying power for up to one-quarter of the twenty-five million Iraqis, so the Marines lived with the constant hum of the powerful turbines as they churned out energy. Occasionally, a rocket or mortar attack would drown out the *hummmm*.

Grant's last move took place on Thanksgiving Day when he transferred to Camp Hit. The Humvee that delivered him to the camp also carried pies for the troops, and the Marines were elated at having a delicious piece of pie for Thanksgiving dinner.

Grant described his new "home" as being like an old jail cell: a tiny concrete room with two lockers, two small beds, and one window. He and his roommate put sandbags over it, so that when a mortar hit outside, it wouldn't blow the glass into the room, but the Browns flag hung proudly over that window, and the carpets we sent earlier were on the floor.

Communication was so much better than in previous wars. My mother-in-law told how, during World War II, it took weeks to get a letter from her husband, who was with the Marines in the Solomon Islands. Her only information came from following the newspaper articles written by war correspondent Ernie Pyle. When my husband was in Vietnam in 1969, we never had a chance to talk "live." We sent audiotapes back and forth, each taking a week or longer to arrive. With Grant, however, we had daily e-mails and an occasional phone call that gave us instant, although momentary, assurance of his well-being. We also received weekly updates from his reserve unit, and this also gave us comfort.

The untold story of war involves those at home who are there for those who have deployed. The stress on families and loved ones cannot be described. I believe that our support for the troops is a great comfort to our men and women in the military, but we also need a support system for those waiting and worrying back home. I worried all the time. My biggest concern was for Grant's safety. I worried about the safety of the men he was responsible for. Not only were they in our hearts and prayers constantly for their own sake, but also for the peace their safety would bring my son.

I never watched the news or read articles in the paper about the war. I couldn't take the chance of knowing the hazards Grant faced. I did read all I could about Iraq's terrain and culture, though, to better understand his situation.

In March 2005, Grant's girlfriend, my husband, and I were thrilled to welcome his reserve unit home in Austin. They were greeted by a full Marine Corps reception. The March On of the colors, the ceremonial presentation of the standards, or flags, was dramatic. Even the governor of Texas was there to welcome them. What a relief! Grant was finally back and safe. The celebration by all who had waited at home for their Marines was euphoric!

Sadly, Grant's Austin unit lost three men, with several others critically wounded. The unit that replaced Grant's in Iraq was the 3rd Battalion, 25th Marines, from Brook Park, Ohio. They did not fare as well, and suffered a sizable number of causalities. My soul wept each time I heard that one of them had been killed. I ache with every parent that has lost a child in the war.

Recently, the Marine Corps flag that has flown in our yard since Grant declared the Marines as his choice after graduation from the Naval Academy in 1994 has been taken down. After four years at the academy and fourteen years as a Marine, Grant has decided to give up the single life and join the girl he met at a language school in Germany on his first deployment. They are currently living in New York City, where he is attending Columbia University and studying for his master's degree.

Elaina Goodrich has been elected to four terms as a township trustee overseeing police, fire service, roads, zoning, cemeteries, and parks. Her responsibilities include being the editor of the quarterly newsletter to the ten thousand residents she proudly serves. She and her husband, George, have two children and are grandparents.

What's a Mother to Do?

Noël Burr

MY STORY BEGINS WHEN I got married to a brand-new second lieutenant in the Army. Ralph had just graduated from West Point. I knew that it meant a life of uniforms and moves and separations, but I never thought of war. That happened in the movies and was over in ninety minutes.

The reality of war became part of our lives in less than two years with multiple deployments to Vietnam. I was left with four small children to care for, but that is another story. I am not a stranger to deployments, and I know that it does not get easier each time. Maybe it gets harder, because each time you have more of a sense of what is happening.

The children grew up through the many moves and school changes and went off to college. Two daughters entered ROTC (the Reserve Officers' Training Corps). We were proud of their dedication, and Ralph was eventually asked to administer the oath of office on graduation to a new Army helicopter pilot and an Air Force public affairs officer.

And then it happened. We got the call. "Mom, I am being deployed to Desert Storm." It was December of 1990 and everything turned to slow motion. Now our daughter, Kathy, was going to war as part of her aviation unit. Our daughter was going to war! Isn't that a male thing? She was a tiny little blue-eyed, blond, wispy-haired baby who, as a young woman, had to get a waiver to be a helicopter pilot because she is so short. And she was going to war! I wanted to be there with her to give her a hug and wave goodbye as she departed, but she was leaving from her post in Germany. What's a mother to do? I could not read the newspaper or listen to or watch the news because it made me anxious. Every time I heard mention of the war, I said a prayer. I prayed a lot during the deployments. Communication was snail mail. Finally she was home and safe.

And then it happened again. "Mom, I am being deployed to Kuwait." This time it was April of 2003. It was the very day her brother Michael was getting married. She was a bridesmaid in absentia. I asked the priest to say a special prayer for her. Kathy would not be flying this time, but scheduling flights for those who were. Again I turned to prayer at the mention of the war. And now communication was e-mail—what a great invention! I spent my days in front of the computer hoping for a message about the heat, the sand, any contact with Kathy, or the USO (United Service Organizations) boxes that were sent from here for all the men and women to share. I worked with the USO shipping out boxes by the dozens to all the military we had addresses for. It helped being a part of the effort to support the troops. And then she was home and safe.

But then there was another deployment. This time Kathy's husband, David, was going to Baghdad. It was February of 2006 just four months after they were married. She knew what it was all about, and we prayed. More USO boxes.

In May of 2007, our son, Michael, called and said, "Mom, Sandy [his wife] is being deployed to Baghdad." She was leaving two-year-old twins. They needed a nanny, so I called the nanny school in our town. The school said that they would help in any way they could for this military deployment. And they did. I was happy that at least I could help them make that connection. The nanny was a lifesaver for my son, who was left with the children, and for me too, because I knew that all was well taken care of at home. Their community in California has an organization that makes quilts for the children of deploying military, and a square of each child's quilt is sent to the parent as a way of keeping them connected. Now communication was daily e-mail to home, including videos so Sandy's children could see Mommy with the Elmo she took with her to Iraq. One early message to us was

> Lots of birds, a nice reminder of the gentle forces of nature, hearing a songbird vs. the bombs in the distance.

We have been alerted that our son-in-law, David, will be deploying again. He will be going to Afghanistan in early 2009. This will be the eighth deployment for me. When will it stop? Will my grandson, Thomas, be the next to go? He just graduated from the Air Force Academy. The president was there and shook hands with each and every one of the more than one thousand graduates and wished them all well as they go to serve their country.

We are the wives, the mothers, the grandmothers. Our uniform is an apron that has a pocket full of hankies. Our deployment happens every time our loved ones leave home. Our mission is to keep the lines of communication open and full of stories and cheer and a few cookies. We have the yellow ribbons on the mailbox so everyone who passes knows and remembers to say a prayer. We serve our country too. We are brave. God bless the troops and the families who wait for them.

Noël Burr is a self-described "military camp follower," with fifteen moves in all. She "joined" the Army when she married her husband, Ralph, then a new graduate of the U.S. Military Academy. She and her husband have four children: two girls and twin boys. She regularly works as a volunteer.

His Choice, Our Pride

Laurie Goyetche

BEFORE OUR SON ZACH was to leave for Marine Corps boot camp, I needed to know: Why, why, why was he choosing to do so at this most dangerous time, and of all the branches, why the Marine Corps? He cited a few reasons, such as "I need more discipline," "my life needs to be put into perspective," and "I will be doing a lot of things I've always wanted to do"—none of which I was willing to accept as a trade-off for the challenges and risks that I knew lay before him.

We had been discussing this with him for three years, but when high school graduation arrived, so did his date for Marine Corps boot camp. We lost the battle. On August 21, 2006, off he went.

Feeling lost and defeated, I turned to my ever-reliable confidants—the moms from a military support group called Marine Moms Online. Did I ever expect to get such an outpouring of responses to my questions? Without a doubt I knew they would come through for me, but was I ready and willing to once again reacquaint myself with the power of this group? You see, I am speaking now of son number two, who is following in the footsteps of his brother, Nick, a former Marine.

Having had one year off between having two sons in service

with the Marines was like a break in the clouds. The storm had passed; the calm was welcomed. My first son returned safely—sound in mind, body, and soul. I was thankful. And I was proud of him and his service. And I rejoiced that there would be no more news reports to fret over, no more calendar countdowns marking his return, no more stalking the mailman for a much-prayed-for letter from my soldier (there were no Internet cafes over there during the 2003 and 2004 deployments).

So indeed I did welcome the power of cyberspace and the moms of Marine Moms Online for round two with our second Marine son's enlistment. Their wealth of information as well as that of another military support group I formed—for moms of Marines in my son's battalion—lent round-the-clock support via e-mails sharing news from our sons' phones calls, photos e-mailed home, and, most important of all, empathy when needed. From this I learned the true meaning of compassion and support, and how to be proudest when the fears were hardest to bear.

Although I already knew the answer to my question—"Why does my son want to be a Marine?"—I knew it would be very interesting to learn why others' sons chose to become Marines. I posted the question to the group. My in-box was quickly flooded with replies from these moms across America sharing their stories. As I read the close to one hundred replies, the pride these parents put forth in writing about their sons found me sitting taller and taller in my computer chair. The more I read, the more I felt myself becoming so tall I might as well have been standing—to salute each and every one of their brave warriors, and these parents, for raising children of such caliber.

Ours is an elite breed of kids. They are young men and women who do not stand behind their flag; they stand in front of it, risking their lives, while putting their parents' emotions in peril alongside them. As they fight for what they believe in, these soldiers are steadfast in protecting the freedoms not only of their nation, but of people in faraway lands. They've relinquished the privileges of their eighteen- to twenty-two-year-old peers and instead learned about life in a way that neither they nor anyone else could imagine.

My experience with both of my sons' military choices and the people I've met along the way these past seven years have changed my life. I've learned through my sons what sacrifice means. I've learned more than ever to be a positive thinker so as to stay on a positive note with my fellow support moms, and hopefully to transmit positive thoughts to my sons at moments when they may most need them to carry on. I realize that without warning, we too could become one of the very unfortunate families that suffer the ultimate loss. If it happened to my son, then I would have to struggle within my gut, but I could not be angry. These are the things military parents think about in their darkest moments, and we realize that we could not strike out and place blame, as that would dishonor our son and those who served beside him.

Attitude—it's all about attitude. From negative and disheartening thoughts positives can be born. The support I received launched my desire to lend support to others. Forming intimate Web groups with the moms of my sons' battalions, and later creating military photo displays for the two communities in which I lived during my sons' enlistments, has been my way to show support for our troops, their families, and my sons.

Displaying the photos of the fine men and women of our community who are serving has made our residents aware of their deployed neighbors—those sacrificing every day for the American way of life. These honorary displays spur conversation among residents and their children about what freedom means. These brave men and women are America's true heroes, even though they themselves don't think so. [The military photo displays are located in the North Olmsted recreation complex and the Broadview Heights community building.]

It took me by surprise, becoming a military mom, which strapped me onto a roller-coaster ride like no other. They say, "Our sons enlist, but we [parents] are drafted." How true it is! Being a military mom has been a life-altering experience with lots of fear and pride and the constant feat of balancing these two very powerful emotions.

Our oldest son, Corporal Nick Jeske, USMC, married his wife just before his second deployment in February 2004. He has been discharged since September 2005. He and his wife bought a home just one year ago (thanks to the VA loan backup benefit) and are enjoying the freedoms of American life that he once fought for. Nick works as a hydraulics mechanic, the skill set he learned as a Marine, but currently is on light duty after an injury to his left hand that left him with extensive nerve damage, with severe loss of sensation and fine motor skills in that hand. He is eligible for permanent disability for this injury but is struggling with having to give up his job and the reality of having to retrain and to redirect his career.

My husband and I were, in part, sustained during our son's combat duty by believing in fate. We held fast to that belief, and luckily our son's fate did bring him home from Iraq (twice) 100 percent sound of mind, body, and soul. When the hand injury occurred in March of 2008 we then knew for sure that you didn't have to be in Iraq or any war zone to sustain injury and life-altering circumstances. His hand was crushed in a forklift truck, and although he is making slow progress it will never be the same.

My message to parents with children serving is that as parents we worry for their safety every day, from the day they are born to the day we die. Just because they go to war does not mean they will be killed or injured. We wake up every day not knowing what will happen to us. Fate can change things in a moment. Through the support of family and friends we sustain that which life deals us. We know that Nick's fortitude and his determination to regain mobility and motor skills in his hand are due at least in part to his being a United States Marine. He has learned that any obstacle can be conquered, and this is just one more test of his ability to do just that.

Corporal Zack Goyetche, USMC, married his wife just before his first deployment in October 2007. She awaited his safe return from Iraq, which was on Mother's Day of 2008! (Undoubtedly, this was the best Mother's Day gift I ever got!) Finally, the two of them are together living in an apartment just outside of Camp Lejeune. We have two more years and at least one more anticipated deployment to go through with Zack. His military occupation recently changed from handling mortars to being a sniper, which he describes himself as hating and loving at the same time; the challenges are tremendous, paralleled only by the rewards.

Creating a Military Photo Display for the Community

To create a photo display, first seek out a spot in any community building that receives a lot of local traffic. Present your idea to the proper authorities. Advertise your project goals, starting with the families of those you know are serving from your community. Then advertise in the high school newsletter and your city's community paper or cable channel. If you see a home that has a yellow ribbon or military flag, or a vehicle parked at a local store with Support Our Troops magnets on it, leave a flyer informing them that you are collecting photos and bio-sketches of the deployed residents of your city. On the flyer, include the information you need them to fill out and your contact information. They can mail or e-mail the photos and information back to you.

Your display can be as simple or complex as you desire. You can attach a foam board to a wall displaying wallet-size photos with each soldier's name and branch of service. If you are computer savvy and want to do more, you can scan the photos and place a detailed military bio-sketch next to each photo. Print it in color, attach it to a piece of colored poster board as a frame, and you have a beautiful entry for your display.

Display enhancements can include a written entry explaining why the military display has been created and what it represents; include four-by-six-inch service branch flags for Army, Navy, Air Force, Marines, and Coast Guard. You may also include an American flag in your display, as well as a Blue Star Service Banner. To honor our fallen soldiers, a Gold Star Service Banner and a framed entry listing the name, service branch, and location and date of death can be presented.

Include a framed entry that tells the viewers what the Blue Star and Gold Star banners represent. For additional interest include extra photos of the soldiers while serving or with family members.

Laurie Goyetche is the proud mother of two Marine sons. She and her husband, Phil, both strongly support the choice their sons made to serve. Both focus on the positive and believe, like their sons, that they can handle anything that lies before them. Laurie and Phil like riding their Harley, especially to Marine functions. Laurie sends letters of support to new Marine recruits, helps moms connect to one another, and creates family websites to help unify military families.

Letting Go

Pat Radva

I PRAYED FOR STRENGTH, HOPE, and forgiveness for my selfishness. My son was being sent overseas to fight for freedom and human rights in another nation, another culture. He had just turned nineteen. My heart burst with pride and yet it was breaking at the same time. It was like reliving his first day in kindergarten all over again. Letting go. I thought about making bargains with God, but I knew better. Let my boy be safe. Ringing phones took on a different sound; was this the dreaded call? Seeing men in their military dress uniform made the hair on the back of my neck stand on end; were they coming to see me? Even in sleep, I found no rest.

I tried to find my son in the videos on TV. I read all the Army articles online, watching for his name. I listened in silent support of our troops and was angered by arguments making moot political points about the whys of the war. I never wavered in my prayers for my son and always included all the warriors. My son and most of his unit returned home. I was both saddened and overjoyed. I could breathe easier and sleep deeper, my prayers answered.

Before I can get too used to him being back at base, off he goes for a second tour. I am very uneasy with this one. I've heard his stories, felt his pain, cried when he should have, and exploded with pride for him. Again, I question the idea of bargains with God. Instead, I hear "Trust in Me." I lose myself in His trust.

There are many weeks when we have no word from Rudy. He calls them "blackouts," which means no external communication. I know this is bad. Really bad. What is happening? Check the Internet and watch the biased TV, searching. Then the call from him comes in—tears of relief that he doesn't hear, and thanks to God that I'm sure He heard. All the support in the world isn't enough to hold me up every day so I can carry on until we hear from Rudy and he comes home again. I function on trust alone. My mind wanders at times from fear, anxiety, and frustration. It is hard to pull it together. I feel so vulnerable and alone. Then he calls. He is okay. I try to keep the talk light and then I don't want to hang up. Just say anything to hear his voice. Time marches on. He makes it home again, safe and sound.

Merry Christmas. He is home for the first time in three years, but the call comes again. Get back to base, we are shipping out on January for six more months. Wait—this is my time with him now. He can't go yet. I am overruled. He leaves two days after Christmas and by January 4 is back in the battle zone in Iraq. I have to let him go again.

Then the call comes—he's been extended until the end of the year, and then for three more months after that. I had a countdown calendar. Four hundred and how many days? This can't be happening again. It is. Trust. I need to get back to that place of trust, so I can function.

I talk about my soldier to everyone. I don't care if they tire of it. It keeps him alive and safe in my mind. Most friends are compassionate and listen. My prayers are consumed with his unit's safety. I try to find fairness with my thoughts for my children at home. It is very hard.

Trust. In June, his R & R is granted and he came home for two weeks. He looks wonderful! He is thinner and more grown up than when I last saw him, but nonetheless healthy. He speaks of what he wants to do when he comes home again as his commitment is near an end. I wanted to stuff him in my mattress with the rest of my valuables and not let him go back.

Overruled again. Driving him to the airport to go back to war is the hardest thing I hope I ever have to do. I am dead inside. I can't say goodbye. I can't kiss his face enough; I beg for promises of phone calls when he can and to please, please, please be safe. My son, who is now a man with unimaginable responsibilities, leaves. He walks tall and proud. I can't look beyond the floor. My shoulders heave from the crying. I finally run out of tears in the evening.

I get back to the countdown. Try to carry on. Trust. It is fifteen months, but to me it feels like fifteen years. I could tell you what happened every single one of those days. I pray and I try to carry on. I put one foot in front of the other and keep going. Finally, he is home. More tears, kisses, and hugs. He allows me this. We both know that we both deserve it. He wants to be helpful. He is respectful, proud, modest, and thankful. He spends time at home with the family, all of us together. Thank you, Lord. He made it and so did I, although I don't think either one of us really came through it all unscathed. Though this, I trust, we can deal with.

Pat Radva was born the fifth of six children to wonderful parents who taught her to be strong and independent. She earned a college degree and has been married to her husband, Rudy, for twenty-eight years. Her goal in life is to leave her mark in this world with the development and success of her four children. She has not been disappointed.

The Call

Linda Tondola

I KNOW THAT MANY OF our military personnel made their decision to join the service after 9/11, but my son Michael had wanted to be a soldier, or "army guy," since he was just a little boy. It wasn't until he was a senior in high school and had talked to several recruiters from different branches of the military that he decided to become a Marine. I met with his recruiter, and although I never tried to stand in Michael's way, many of his friends and relatives did try to change his mind. They asked me why I was letting him do this. But I knew, as only a mother does, that this wasn't just what he wanted to do, it was what he had to do.

Michael was not very fond of school. He hated homework. He hated sitting in a classroom. Every year of school ended with him barely passing. Michael was smart; he just didn't want to apply himself. When he decided to join the Marines, he had to apply himself. His recruiter constantly checked up on him and made sure that he put schoolwork first. I thought, "Maybe this isn't so bad." Because Michael would only be seventeen when he graduated from high school, I had to give parental consent for him to enlist. At first, I wasn't sure I should do it. Maybe I should wait and let him enlist on his own when he turned eighteen in the fall.

I knew he would just be biding his time until he could leave. I knew that in the big picture, a few months wouldn't matter. Remember, this was what he had wanted all his life.

And so just two weeks after graduation from high school, my only son and youngest child—my baby—left the nest and went to boot camp. Our lives have never been the same since. I was promised that I would send away a boy and get back a man. They were right. When twelve long weeks had passed, I watched that young man—still seventeen years old, mind you—graduate from boot camp and become a United States Marine. It was one of the proudest moments of my life.

Less than a year later, that young man was in Iraq. I'll never forget the morning I was awakened by the phone. He had been there less than a month, and he called to tell me that the Humvee he had been driving was hit by an IED. Michael was okay, but he had a concussion. My heart broke when he told me that his vehicle commander, who had been sitting only inches away, was killed. Michael was eighteen when the accident occurred and he was awarded a Purple Heart for injuries he received.

Here I was, a new Marine mom, new to this whole deployment thing, and I get news like that after the first month he's deployed! The online support groups had assured me that he would be okay! Why did this happen? I had heard of survivor guilt; I had "mother of survivor guilt," even though I knew the accident wasn't his fault. My faith in God increased by leaps and bounds that year. There literally was nothing I could do but pray for him.

That first deployment, I couldn't tear myself away from news of the war. TV. Newspapers. Radio. Internet. I had to know. It was a way that I could be there in my heart even if I couldn't be there physically. I learned with his second deployment not to pay attention to the media, as they never reported any of the good things going on. Michael was in a safer place this time, but he was also in more remote areas. The longest I went without hearing from him was seven weeks. He was constantly moving from base to base, but at least the newsletters from the unit's support group were promising. Things were good. The people were friendly.

Michael just finished his second deployment to Iraq. He arrived back in the United States on Mother's Day of this year. It was the best Mother's Day I've ever had! Fortunately, this deployment was "uneventful." Well . . . with the exception that Michael decided to reenlist in the Marines. How do I feel about that? I am so very proud of him. The decision he made all those years ago was the right one for him. He loves being a Marine. He loves the excitement. He's good at what he does, and he is a fine young man.

Do I miss him? Oh, so much! I am still learning to accept this life, still learning to cope with having a child who is so far away that I can't just jump in my car and go see him. When I want to talk to him, I have to wait for him to call, because there's no phone where he is. I am learning that silence is a good thing. No news is good news.

I cry when I hear about a local Marine or soldier who was killed. It could be my son. I check the license plates of cars parked in front of my house to make sure they aren't military plates and there aren't two Marines waiting there for me when I come home from work. When I don't recognize the caller ID, I still answer it—Michael might be calling home. When he is in the States, I can sleep at night. When he is deployed, I pray at night.

Michael, at twenty years of age and has been a Marine for three years now. (Is he really only twenty?) He was married last year. He's lived a lifetime in the past few years. One thing for sure, his life will never be dull. And because of him, neither will mine. My son is Corporal Michael Garlock, stationed in Camp Lejeune, North Carolina. He is with the 3rd Battalion, 2nd Marines, Weapons Company.

Linda Tondola is a registered nurse who works in a nursing home. She and her husband, Mike, together have six children—three each—and two granddaughters. She enjoys reading and being active.

April Fool's Day

Jayne White

I WAS SO PROUD WHEN my son, Matthew Meyrose, told me that he joined the Army. (He enlisted on April 1, 2004, no joke.) After his basic training, Combat Engineer became his MOS (military occupational specialty), which means he built bridges, placed and detonated explosives, and looked for bombs. This training and the schedule of his unit kept him in the States for a year and a half. Then came Matthew's deployment to Afghanistan on March 3, 2006.

I had mixed feelings about him leaving the country. Guilt because I suggested he join the Army, apprehension, then calm as I prayed for him and all those serving. I bought a passport right away; I figured if I had it, I wouldn't need it.

I would receive calls from him at work. Everyone would be quiet so that I could hear him better. The time delay on the phone is a little hard to get used to. You want to ask questions and your soldier just wants to hear your voice. You end up talking over each other, so I would count to three and then speak. He sounded so close. Of course, they never tell you much, to keep your fear at a minimum.

Then came the call, at 8:30 A.M. on Saturday April 1, 2006 (April

Fool's Day—no joke again). Not even a month out of country, Matthew was wounded and in the hospital. An IED went off under his Humvee. His wife didn't have much information, but was told he wasn't critical. Matthew (twenty-four at the time) had short-term memory loss and his right arm had a muscle concussion. Luckily for him, he is left-handed.

In the meantime, I joined a group called Blue Star Mothers of America, Inc. (A flag with a blue star emblazoned in the center is the sign of a child in the service.) They support our troops, our veterans, and each other. Attending their support groups and meeting with Matthew's recruiter helped me.

It took four months of trial and error to realize that his arm needed more than just time to heal. Matt was flown to Germany to receive medical attention. The timing was perfect, as Matt's uncle Hugo, also in the Army serving in Kuwait, was on leave in Germany that week. My sister was meeting Hugo for two weeks, and the three of them went out to dinner. I instructed her to hug Matthew nonstop for me. Matthew came home August 30, 2006, and did the rest of his time at Fort Drum, New York. Mathew's three years and seventeen weeks were up September 30, 2007, and he was a sergeant by the time he was done serving. He is now going to school to be a fireman and is a drill sergeant in the Army Reserves.

Jayne White's favorite colors are red, white, and blue, and it's easy to see why: She was born on base at Cherry Point, North Carolina, while her father was a Marine; her grandfather was an Army engineer in World War I; both of her sisters served (one met her husband while in Germany in the Army Band); and her husband, Wayne, (Matt's step-father) was also in the Army. Retired after working thirty-five years at a bank, Jayne volunteers at the USO and Red Cross.

Waiting for E-mails

Diane Berlin

AFTER VIETNAM, I PRAYED for daughters only. I could never handle one of my children being in harm's way. Daughter, daughter, and then son. Oh well, there is no draft. Thank God I am safe!

Eric turned eighteen and four days later he was gone to the Marines. All his buddies wished the recruiter good luck with Eric's mom. Eric said, "I feel the need to serve my country as my father, uncle, and grandfathers before me." I could not believe my ears. The one thing I did not want my son to have to do, and he felt the need to choose to serve. I could not catch my breath. I felt like he had just up and disappeared—vanished, leaving a huge hole in my life. I would have taken his place if I could. The day before he left he asked me, "How do you turn on the washing machine?" I realized I had not prepared him for life on his own. I always wanted to be there and take care of him, at least for now!

We went to Eric's graduation from boot camp. I was so proud of all the young people marching in front of us with such precision. Knowing each one was someone's child pulled at my heart strings. During the ceremony the Leatherneck award was presented to the person with the highest marksmanship points. The next name announced was Eric Berlin. This shocked me. He never went hunting. My husband served in Vietnam and, after the treatment of the troops coming home, never owned a gun. Our baby boy, who we dedicated to God before he was one, is now a tall, handsome young man and a Marine. It seems like I had only blinked for a moment!

Eric came home for a visit, which is never long enough. He left for additional training at Fort Leonard Wood, or as people kindly refer to it, Fort Lost in the Woods. Several weeks later, Eric called. "Mom, as of tomorrow, I can come home for a visit." It was too late to make reservations, so I hurriedly looked up his location on MapQuest. The travel time was nine hours. I would drive to the ends of the earth to pick him up if necessary! I told him, "I'll be there."

We had a wonderful visit and then our time was up. We had to return Eric to the airport Easter Sunday so that he could be at his new home base in Hawaii the next day. I did not know when we would get to see each other again. Oh well, I thought, he will be safe.

The day after he got there he called me. "Mom, I'm leaving for Iraq this week."

Eric knew he was leaving when he was home, but he did not want us to be upset. Again, I couldn't catch my breath! It had only been eight months since he turned eighteen. I felt like I was in a horror show. How can a person be prepared in eight months to face life-and-death situations?

Before Eric left for boot camp, I cut one little curl of his hair off his head—with much difficulty (in fact, the recruiter got it for me). I placed that curl in a special locket I bought. When Eric went to Iraq, I wore it the whole time. I did not know I had so many tears in me. This was such a difficult time for the whole family. My husband's thoughts drifted back to Vietnam. He became very withdrawn.

When Eric was in Iraq, we were able to correspond by e-mails.

Thank God! I have saved them all. Every word from him I cherished. He would not share with me what his job was. He just told me, "You do not want to know." Yet, I felt compelled to read everything I could about what was going on over there. I listened to the news constantly and I couldn't sleep. I felt like a huge part of my heart was missing. I tried not to mention it to anyone in the family, because I did not want them to worry. I started taking medicine for anxiety.

Wednesday, May 9, the first e-mail arrived!

> hey mom, there is a lot of stuff going on here so i wont have a lot of time to get on the computer and stuff but i will try my best, i just wanted to tell you i made it here safe and tell dad i said the C130 (troop and cargo transport aircraft) ride sucked especially cuz it was like 120 degrees !! love you all.

Now my life revolved around the computer. A few short sentences could make my day or week.

Tuesday, May 15:

> hey, sorry bout not callin to wish you a happy mothers day . . . all the internet and phones were out . . . the spot we are in does not have a mailing thing set up yet but we are taking a convoy to another base tomorrow . . . I'm not really in a stationary place, I'm security for civilian contractors and just drive then around where they need to go . . . love you a lot

Friday, June 14:

> hey dad, i just will always know how good we have it back home . . . even if the cavs dont win lol but yea i have to get to chow in a minute but i tried to call earlier today at about

1030 here but just got the answering machine . . . i will talk
to you later pops

Slowly the days passed, but with the Internet we were able to keep in touch. One e-mail from Eric started a strange chain of events. On July 19, Eric wrote an e-mail regarding his car and the trouble he had with it before he left. Jokingly he said, "Tell Dad to buy an El Camino and I will trade him, I have always wanted one and will probably not be able to find one." I went on eBay and found a 1978 El Camino, forwarded the information to Eric, and said jokingly, "When you get ready to buy one, look on eBay."

Friday, July 27:

can you look through my papers from my bank navy fed and
get my checks . . . i need the first and last group of numbers
in the very bottom of the front of the check. i need them so i
can sign up for paypal and pay for the el camino, and i asked
tressa to find someone to pick it up for me. can you get this
address to her and she can mapquest it to get directions . . . .
thnx mom, love you and be safe!!!
this is the phone number to the place and address and the guy
that runs it. please call him and tell him that it can get picked
up, he thinks i'm lyin to him.

The next thing you know my husband and I are making a two-hundred-mile trip to pick up a car Eric had purchased sitting in the middle of Iraq!

There were many boxes of goodies sent to Eric and his platoon. Eric loves to play basketball and in one of his e-mails he indicated he still played there:

yea i had an ingrown toe nail that i kinda had to cut out of my foot . . . it hurt really bad for a few days but now its all better, i can play basketball again, haha yes i still play out here even though its really hot . . . me and some guys i work with built up a little hoop that we can play on, i made sure it was regulation and every thing lol we are always building random stuff out of wood.

Again I jumped at the opportunity to try and bring some normality to the troops. My husband and I immediately went to a sports store and purchased a basketball, hoop net, football, and a hand pump. As my husband was deflating the basketball, he found it very surreal that he was sending an Ohio State basketball made in Vietnam to his son fighting in Iraq. How ironic is that? The sports equipment was a big hit.

July 30:

but yea we have used both of the balls you sent me, mostly the football cuz more people can play that, it makes you feel like home.

Eric turned nineteen in Fallujah, Iraq. How do you celebrate when he is not even home? I wanted so much to bake him a cake and hug him! I wanted to make his day special. I asked everyone I knew to send him a funny birthday card.

September 14:

haha its alright mom, you can just do what they make us do and carry a little note pad around and write everything you need to remember down haha works pretty well actually and yes i think i got most of the birthday cards and the boxes from the boy scouts, tell everyone i said thank you very much and

> kindness like that is what helps me get up every morning out here, knowing that there are good people back home that are counting on all of us out here . . . i passed out a lot of the stuff to the guys and the woopie cushion was a big hit haha
> love you mom

I felt so out of control, a feeling I don't like at all. My days consisted of waiting for an e-mail to pop up at work and then I would cry. One day my boss walked by and wanted to know if I was okay because tears were running down my face. I said these were tears of joy because Eric e-mailed me in between missions and he had just gotten in. I was riding an emotional roller coaster and I was not in charge of anything. I had to put everything in God's hands. This made me realize that I cannot control anything but me. I have learned to let little things go.

When Eric got home from Iraq, I was very thankful. I had asked God to wrap his arms around him and bring him home safely. Thank You, God! He was home. I could handle this after all. It would be easier the next time, or so I was telling myself.

Now the time is approaching for his return to Iraq. Even though it is three months away, I am already starting to cry for no reason. It is not easier the next time. I have come to the conclusion that any time your child is in danger, it tears at your very soul. It tests your faith and makes you wonder if you are worthy of another miracle. It makes you connect with your every nerve. I am so proud of Eric I could just explode, yet I am so very afraid of losing him. It makes you wonder if he knows how much he is loved and cared about. Did I make him too patriotic? I always told my husband that I was glad I did not know him when he was in Vietnam because I could never have lived through it. Did I not convey that to my son enough? And yet I must respect his wishes to serve and protect. I am so very proud of the young man he has become, and yet each time he faces combat I fall apart inside. As departure time again approaches, I realize that God is in charge and he has blessed me with a wonderful son.

EDITORS' NOTE: Diane Berlin and her husband, Fred, were instrumental in pointing out a specific need of local military families to reporter Bob Dyer and the *Akron Beacon Journal*'s readers. No branch of the military will pay to fly its soldiers to their hometowns, only their home base. After that, our soldiers are on their own to pay for tickets to reach home. Because service people don't know the exact dates for their leaves until the last minute, airline fares are extremely high. The solution to the problem is the newly created Airfare Assistance Fund helping local families of service members who want to come home right before shipping out to Iraq or Afghanistan, or those returning from a tour of duty. The third option for aid from the fund is for families flying to a U.S. airport to meet their deceased soldier. For assistance with airline tickets or to give a tax-deductible donation, please call New Covenant Community Church at 330-253-6989. The fund was a big help assisting Eric with his visit home before his current tour of duty.

Diane Berlin has worked for a health care provider for more than twenty-five years. She has three children and two grandchildren, a black Labrador retriever, and an African Tong Tortoise. Her father served in the Air Force. ("I should have known!" she says.) Her husband, Fred, served in the Marines. She married Fred twenty-two years ago and loves him as much as she did on the day she married him.

You Are on My Mind and in My Heart Always

Elsie

It shouldn't have come as a surprise, and yet it did. When I met my son at Max and Erma's for lunch his announcement still took my breath away. We had talked for several years about this, but I thought he would finish college first. That was not going to happen now, because between bites of salmon salad came the announcement that he had enlisted in the Army. He wanted me to be the first to know and asked me not to tell his father or his brother until he had passed his physical and was sure it was official. I kept my promise and his secret. For three weeks, I alternated between sadness and pride. My tender, intelligent, analytical, and brutally honest son had followed what was in his heart and joined the service with full knowledge that in doing so he would be at war.

His father, brother, and I brought him to the MEPS (Military Entrance Processing Station), where he officially became a soldier in the Army of the United States of America. He would be a private first class in the infantry. His test scores had qualified him for more exotic duties, but he wanted to be a grunt on the front lines. His basic training was at Fort Benning in Columbus, Georgia. It was summer, hot and humid, and he almost became a heat casualty. His drill sergeant saw to it that he made up all the classes he missed when he was in the infirmary. In November of 2005 with hearts full of love and pride, his father, brother, sister-in-law, grandmother, mother, and assorted aunts, uncles, and cousins witnessed his graduation from basic training. His first assignment was Fort Lewis in Washington State; after that he was sent to Vilseck, Germany. In August of 2007 he deployed to Iraq. I don't feel I have taken a really deep breath since.

My first thought when he was deployed was that I didn't want him to think he was forgotten, so I would e-mail or write every day. All my letters or e-mails are signed the same way: "I love and miss you; you are on my mind and in my heart always. MOM"

I send packages at least once a month. I enlisted relatives, friends, and neighbors to e-mail, write, or send care packages, too. I have made batches of pizelles (Italian waffle cookies) to send to my son and a friend. The hardest times are holidays. This Christmas, my son's unit was in the process of moving to a new COB (Contingency Operating Base) and his address changed. The Christmas package I mailed December 15 got there at the end of January. For his birthday, I sent him a cake through a company called Bake Me a Wish! (accessible online)—it got there ten days after his birthday. The hardest part for a mother to endure during a deployment is not knowing. When it has been three weeks since you got an e-mail, letter, or phone call, your mind works overtime. It was during one of those no-news periods, on my way home from work, I heard on the radio that three soldiers were killed by an IED in Iraq. I immediately was overcome by the irrational fear that my son was one of the soldiers, and I was terrified of going home. I was fearful that when I pulled into the driveway, soldiers would be there to deliver the news. Then my son called, and all the irrational fears melted away and I was relieved. During these calls, I try to glean through my son's words, through his voice—the way he tells me things—if he is okay. I worry as much about his mental health as his physical well-being.

Three months into his deployment, he came home for a two-week leave. I wanted him to decide how to spend those precious days home. He went fishing with his dad and spent a lot of time with his fourteen-month-old nephew, Jake. He also spent a day at the school where I teach. It was Veterans Day and he came to talk to the third-graders about what it means to be a soldier. He had put together a PowerPoint with pictures of his fellow soldiers and pictures of the people and places in Iraq. He made sure that the soldiers he depicted were representative of the diversity of the Army. He talked a lot about how the soldiers respect the people and culture of Iraq, and about how the war was not with them but with those whose only mission was to foster their own ideology through any means. He brought pictures of the Iraqi children and talked about how hard life is for them in a war zone. The third-graders were really moved by the presentation and asked many questions. I had a hard time not crying. I have never been so proud of my son. For the rest of the school year, kids at my school asked about my son, wondered about his safety, and told me stories of their relatives who were also deployed in Iraq.

While my son was on leave, he made a video of my grandson, Jake, who had just learned to walk. Jake was trying to take his dog, JR, a Jack Russell, for a walk. In the video, you can hear my son laughing at the sight of this little guy trying to hold on to the leash and, instead of walking the dog, being walked by the dog. You don't see my son, but the pure joy in his laughter is a precious gift to me. I watch that video whenever sadness overtakes me.

I have found solace in various organizations. The Blue Star Mothers is a nonprofit organization. They send care packages to the troops, visit soldiers at the VA hospitals, attend the funerals of our fallen soldiers, and undertake many other activities to support the enlisted troops. I am also on a blog for mothers of enlisted men and women. All of my friends have been supportive, but it is not the same. It is important to connect with those who have been or are in the same situation now. The best antidote for missing my son is being with my almost two-year-old grandson, Jake. He is my therapy.

My son is now on a COB northeast of Baghdad in a rural area of Iraq. The mosquitoes are horrific, and the soldiers have to burn their body waste. The heat is oppressive, and the air conditioning only works when the generators are operational. Danger from IEDs, snipers, and insurgents is omnipresent. The soldiers are working every day; there is little time off. Through all this hardship, my son has thrived. He has been promoted to sergeant and likes the responsibility that comes with the promotion. His duties include being a commander's gunner, working as a tower guard, handling administration in his unit after duty hours, or CQ (charge of quarters), monitoring an eagle-eye tower (infrared sensor systems and motion detection radars), and driving the mortar truck for nightly missions.

This is not the life I would have chosen for my son. He chose it, so I embrace it. With prayers and the grace of God he will be home. My son is a sergeant in the Army. He has been deployed in Iraq since August 2007 and will be back in Germany in November of 2008.

EDITORS' NOTE: This soldier doesn't want his name mentioned because he thinks that what he is doing isn't that special, that others have done more, and that it's his job.

The Marine, the Paratrooper, and Cancer

Mickie Heaton

HAVING A CHILD SERVING in the military is always daunting; having two sons serving in Iraq at the same time is almost unbearable. For four months in 2006, both of my sons, Kit and Nate, were stationed there. Kit was a lance corporal in the United States Marine Corps and Nate was in the United States Army as a specialist in the 82nd Airborne Division.

My oldest son, Kit, just came home one day and said that he had enlisted in the Marine Corps. He was in the delayed program so that he could go to boot camp at Camp Lejeune, North Carolina, with his good buddy, Joey. He would turn twenty with a drill instructor screaming in his face, and turn twenty-one watching prisoners in a jail in Iraq.

Kit was to be deployed in July 2005, the same month that I was to have a two-pound tumor taken out of my leg, at the knee. I was recovering from the surgery, thinking about my son flying to Iraq, when my husband and two other sons walked into my hospital room. Of course, I was happy to see them, but then Kit peeked around the curtain with a giant bouquet of flowers! My pulse went from 70 to 135 (they told me later) and I just dissolved into tears. He had time to fly back home before he was deployed just to see me, and as I type this the emotions are just right there . . . it was so very sweet. My husband didn't even know.

My projected six-week stay at home turned into six more months in the hospital and seven surgeries! So, while I was dealing with more pain than I had ever known, my eldest son was dodging bullets whizzing through a palm tree in Iraq. While we were singing "Silent Night" on Christmas Eve in a church bathed in candlelight, Kit, we later found out, was engaged in a fierce battle for his life and those of his fellow Marines. Knowing how difficult my Marine's life was made me a stronger woman.

We would hear from Kit sporadically, because he would be on patrol for up to a month at a time. We had to use MotoMail, a relatively new way to communicate, by which I could send an e-mail, it would get printed out and delivered to him, and then he would respond to us when he was able to get to a computer. Every bit of correspondence, no matter how short, was a great comfort to me.

July, 2005
waz up dude its nate
its great to hear from you and do it as offen as you can. also troy left for bootcamp yesterday. that kid is so damn small i think I am a little bit worried about him. its hard to think that hes going to be a soldier. its weird to think that I am going to be a soldier in just a short time. anyways good luck over there . . . we got your back over here while you watch our back over there. And i guess i never said this to you but i guess now is the only way . . . i love you man and iam so proud of you. defend your country well Marine
—Army EAGLE scout
Nate and Mom

Kit's response:

> im starting to read this book, its called "The Dead Room" by Robert Ellis, its pretty good and im reading it pretty fast, you could also send over good books if youd like. To nate . . . yeah troy is a little guy but there is a saying that goes . . . "Its not the size of the dog in the fight, its the size of the fight in the dog," i think he'll do fine, and there is not a doubt in my mind that you won't acomplish your goals, and if anybody gives you shit they gotta answer to me..hahha. what you said at the end of the email hit me pretty hard, it feels good to know you care and to see how our relationship has grown as we've gotten older, love ya bro, talk to you soon
> Love kit

Coping with Kit being in Iraq and with my cancer made me detached, but not too much because Nate was going to Army boot camp in the fall of 2005. My youngest son, Hunter, helped me stay cheerful, at least when he was looking! Hunter kept me strong. I could let my guard down with my husband, but not with the boys. I had, and continue to have, a very strong group of family and friends whose prayers, support, and encouragement helped more than they will ever know. With Kit and Nate praying for me . . . I could not be anything but strong. Though I was going through tremendous pain, it was nothing like what they were experiencing. They were the strong and courageous ones.

When Hunter was in the eighth grade, he submitted an essay as to why he should be picked to place a wreath at the Tomb of the Unknown Soldier. He was picked! These were his words:

> I think I deserve to put the Wreath on the Tomb of the Unknown Soldier . . . Why, because I have two brothers in the Military, Kit my oldest brother is 21, he is in the Marines, he is

also a Lance Corporal. Unfortunately, he is in Iraq right now. He has been there since July, the same month my Mom had surgery for her cancer. Kit will be coming home in February. My other brother Nate just turned 19, he is in Boot Camp right now at Fort Benning, Georgia. He wants to be an Airborne Army Ranger. We will be going to Nate's graduation December 13th. Nate is a Private First Class, he has this rank because he is an Eagle Scout. Ever since Nate was small, he used to play with GI Joe men. He also used to get books on the Civil War, and he likes to paint little Civil War men and write war poems. He was always thinking of going in to the military. So, when he got out of High School he enlisted in the Army. He really wanted to go when September 11th happened. After that incident happened he said, "I decided to join the Army out of patriotism due to the events of September 11th 2001, so that I can do my part to defend this country." Kit really wasn't like that, after a year out of school he got a job, then one day he came home and said he had enlisted in the Marines. We were stunned because we would never have thought. When Kit was still in the house, he always used to beat me up, I couldn't wait until he left. But now that he is in Iraq, I want him to come home, because he is nice to me now. I want both of them to come home. So what I'm trying to say is that I'm grateful that we are free, we wouldn't be here if these brave men had not fought for us and this country and died a hero, you are not forgotten.

Thank you!

"The last full measure of devotion"—Abe Lincoln

Nate was always playing with toy soldiers as a child. He decided at age twelve to go into the military. Going to Fort Benning, Georgia, for boot camp at age nineteen, he too turned twenty-one while patrolling in Iraq. Before he was deployed in December 2006, he was granted a special leave, with the help of the wonderful Red Cross, to come and see me in the hospital. The cancer had gone to my lung, and the spot had to be removed. It was so awesome to have my son with me, even while I was talking complete drug-induced nonsense . . . he just loved that!

So, while Nate was fighting battles that lasted seven hours, or comforting a buddy who lay dying, I was going through three months of grueling chemotherapy while always thinking about him. Toward the end of the treatment, all my numbers were so very low, I had to spend nine more days in the hospital. Hunter was scared and told Nate in an e-mail that he was afraid I was going to die. (I had explicitly told Hunter that he could tell anyone *but* Nate!) I didn't want Nate to worry about me at all. We all had to be so very strong and not give up on the hope that everything would be all right.

Sending packages to the boys was not just a family affair. People whom I did not even know sent them wonderful things . . . . like Skittles, actually, too many Skittles!!

July 22,2007
hey i got the package from santa. it was one of the best packages i have gotten out here. tell them thanks a million.

Whenever the boys called, I always tried to think of something humorous that happened when they were little, or a funny story that made fun of their Dad—that always made them laugh!

When I would worry if I had not heard from Nate in weeks, Kit would always say, "It's good news when you don't hear from him," and of course, he was right. Sometimes, his e-mails contained a little too much info:

May 4, 2007
hey just had a little time to write something. today it got up to 103. its getting crazy hot. you just sweat standing there. o ya you can send me more phone cards and tuna if you want.

love that stuff. pretty boring the last few days. nothing really happening besides mortar attacks. well i am going to go to bed now. love you.
your faithful soldier,
Nathaniel Chabrand Heaton

A lot of people ask me how I did it. I simply try not to think about it too much. When I do, it just makes me sad and proud at the same time. We will always be so very proud of our sons and the courage it took for them to go to war.

October 17, 2007
"freedom is something people enjoy without thinking, soldiers will pay the price for freedom without thinking." . . . Patton
Love nate

Kit has been honorably discharged from the Marine Corps and is currently working and attending college. Nate is at Fort Bragg, North Carolina, and will be deployed to Afghanistan in June of 2009.

Mickie Heaton is a dental assistant in a pediatric dental practice. She married Richard, her high school sweetheart, in 1971 and together they have three children. Mickie is currently cancer free.

Army Mom, Serving in the Silent Ranks

Kathy Sargent

I AM THE MOTHER OF two U.S. Army soldiers and one civilian. I am a member of the "Silent Ranks" here at home. We of the Silent Ranks go about our business every day. We go to the grocery store, take our younger children to dance, soccer, baseball, and band practice. We clean our homes, take care of our yards, cook, and clean. We are the ones with the service banner pins on our collars or coats and with magnetic support ribbons covering our cars. We have tear-stained faces and cry while reading the labels of canned foods at the store. It's just our pressure release valve letting off a little steam when our pressure cooker lives get to be a little too much to deal with. We can be seen in the stores with shopping carts filled with small items that we can stuff into flat-rate shipping boxes to send to our soldiers so far from home. At home we fly the American flag alongside a service banner and another flag representing the branch of military our children serve in. We're just like everyone else; we just have a little more on our minds than most.

Bradley, born in July 1985, a rambunctious child with big brown eyes and blond hair, was always there to lend a helping hand with his baby brother, Andrew, who was born in December of 1986. This is as close as I'd ever want to be to having twins! Bradley always serious and Andrew always joking; there was never a dull moment with them around. They both played the trumpet and played baseball. Brad just took these things a little more seriously than Andy did. But that's not all; they both joined the Army right out of high school.

When Bradley announced his plan to join the Army in 2002, my heart sank. I cried for days and felt completely helpless. How could a good-looking and smart kid make such a big mistake?! And now that he was eighteen, I had no say in what he did. What would I tell his little brother, Timmy? And how was he going to handle this? My hands were tied. Bradley planned to play his trumpet in the Army band, but he had to pass the audition. He was scared, nervous, and unsure of himself, but when the time came, he and his trumpet both rose to the occasion. He got in where he wanted to be.

We all made it through boot camp and Bradley graduated as a specialist. I remember being so proud of him, knowing all he had been through. He had changed, and changed for the better. The boy who went away to boot camp appeared to have grown up in only nine weeks. He was now a man and he had a plan. His plan was to make the Army his career. This had me crying again for a while, and worrying a little more often.

Brad made it through AIT (Advanced Infantry Training), and two Army bases later, he found himself playing funerals and telling us how hard it was. He would travel to play funerals around the country, each one leaving a mark on him and a new respect for the soldiers fighting over in Iraq. This bothered me more than it bothered Brad; he did what he had to do and was good at it.

Before we knew it, Andrew had enlisted. I was devastated!

Not only was he joining, he was going to be a combat medic! He assured me he would be fine, but I remember telling him, well, more like yelling at him, "If you want to know what that's going to be like, let me paint a red cross on your back and shoot at you while you run through the yard!" I was beside myself! How could he do this, knowing how Brad's joining affected me?

Another boot camp graduation in 2005, more tears of pride, and more worry to add to my daily life. Andrew would go to Fort Sam Houston in Texas for AIT courses. Okay. I can deal with that. Then the phone call: "Mom, I'm shipping out to Kuwait." I wanted to die. "You just got out of boot camp! What do you mean you're going to Kuwait? Details, dude, I need details!" He told me not to worry, but I worried anyway, and was always on the phone or e-mailing Brad, trying to understand why my baby was half-way across the world. Brad would say, "At least he's not in Iraq, he's going to be fine!" Andrew was fine—although one of my last phone calls to him was cut a little short by him saying, "Mom, let me call you back. Some jerk is shooting at us at the entrance to the base." He did his job in Kuwait and was ready to head back to Germany for R & R. That was when Bradley announced that he had volunteered to go to Iraq.

I was a basket case. My simple worry had turned into full-blown terror. I remember crying uncontrollably for days. The tears would come and go, and without warning. I couldn't deal with the fact that my baby was willing to walk right into harm's way. I had spent the past years protecting both of them, and now I wondered what I did wrong. Was it the video games we allowed them to play? TV programs? Movies they'd seen? What did I do wrong?

Bradley, a sergeant at age twenty-one, was volunteering his services. Andrew was still expected to go back and spend more time in Kuwait. I was stuck at home and feeling like I was placed in a pressure cooker with no release valve. I was panicking, I was having panic and anxiety attacks, I was snapping at people, crying, screaming . . . I was watching the news, reading everything I could about what was going on in Iraq. Trying to find out how long it would take them to redeploy Andrew and send him there too. I was my own worst enemy. I was scared and felt helpless, and I had no idea what I was supposed to do. Mom is *always* supposed to know what to do! Why do I have absolutely no clue here?!

I started looking for support—anywhere. We all had MySpace pages. I used mine to keep in contact with the boys. I searched there for other moms going through the same thing. I had already talked with one mom who was having a hard time with her son's enlistment. Her son sent her to me, so I thought maybe I could find people like myself to help me. I was introduced to another site, which was a bulletin board full of mothers who sent their children off to serve. I told them what I was going though. Not one of them told me to "suck it up." They all understood. They all sympathized and offered phone numbers and e-mail addresses as support. They all told me that if the stress and depression got too bad, to see a doctor for help, that this was all normal, and we are all in it together. I had finally found my support!

When Bradley was sent to Iraq, I didn't hear from him for weeks, and the stress level here at home was something that nightmares are made of. I couldn't sleep, couldn't work, and couldn't function knowing my son was over there. I still had so many things I wanted to tell him. And all the negative thoughts that would pop into my head were driving me crazy. I went to the bulletin board and I posted my thoughts, feelings, and emotions. I received responses in minutes. These ladies are angels! They help me up, and allow me to hold on to what is left of my sanity! I wasn't alone then, and I'm not alone now. Slowly, Bradley got back online, and we would hear from him once in a while. He had deleted his MySpace page, so I didn't have the security blanket of logging in to see if he had logged on that day any more. But at least he was sending e-mail!

My car is a mobile billboard showing my pride in my boys. Everything from my license plate to the ribbons and bullet-hole stickers to the signs in my back window. But this has caused me some problems as well. I've been spat on and had things thrown at my car. I've been told that my sons are baby killers and other evil things. I have created a box that I take to public functions that I attend. It's painted in desert camouflage and has the words LETTERS FROM HOME painted on the side in army font. I put it out with blank cards for people to fill out, and then I send them to my son for his unit in Iraq. Why not support the boys everywhere I go?!

Birthdays and holidays are rough. For Christmas, we sent care packages to Brad and Andy. They had all kinds of goodies like a string of lights, candy-filled ornaments, some giant glittery snowflakes, a Christmas card, and a couple of fun gifts.

I have stopped watching the news, stopped watching pretty much anything that has to do with the military, and when a car pulls into my driveway at night my heart nearly pounds right out of my chest with fear. All this, just to find out that the car was only turning around. When my phone rings after 10 P.M., I'm afraid to even look to see who is calling, let alone actually answer it. But at the same time, I'm praying that it's Brad calling from Iraq.

I read the newspaper, and can't believe how upset I get when I hear of another soldier being killed. My heart breaks for his mother. I don't want to know what she's going through. I don't want to imagine. I don't want her to hurt either, and there is nothing I can do. To me, the men and women over there in that sandbox are our children first, and soldiers second. I pray for every one of them every night. And when I'm done praying for them, I pray for their parents.

Sergeant Bradley is currently stationed in Iraq. He is supposed to be home in December of 2008 and will go back to Iraq again after his twelve-month leave, for another "vacation at the beach." Specialist Andrew is stationed at Fort Knox. He is working in the

Ireland Army Community Hospital on base. We have no idea when he may be deployed again.

Me? Well, I sit here at home, chatting with other moms online who feel like their hearts have been ripped from their chests. My cat, Army Boots, given to me by my son Bradley, keeps me company; he is in my lap more than he is on the ground. I take my fifteen-year-old son, Timothy, to his baseball games and practice, and I listen to him play the trumpet his brother Bradley gave to him. I dread the day Timothy graduates from high school, because he too is going to enlist in the Army. The day he graduates will be hard. If he's like his brothers, he'll be scared, nervous, and unsure of himself. When the time comes, he will rise to the occasion, because he too will be where he wants to be, just like his brothers—a soldier in the U.S. Army.

Kathy Sargent is the proud mother of three sons. She enjoys woodworking, gardening, watching the wildlife in her backyard, and sending care packages to our troops overseas.

The Milk Bowl

Fran Clark

WHEN OUR SON, CHRISTOPHER, began his freshman year at Miami University in Oxford, Ohio, he decided to join the Navy ROTC program. We were surprised and wondered how he got the inspiration. We thought, if that is what he wants to do, fine, and we'll save some money! As we attended the midshipmen's activities, and especially his commissioning as a second lieutenant in the Marine Corps, we grew more proud and aware of the good people in the military. We became a military family.

His training to become an F/A-18D aviator with the VMFA(AW)-225 Squadron was very exciting, but tough. He was required to undergo SERE (Survival, Evasion, Resistance and Escape) school, which involved survival training, evading capture, and experiencing a POW (prisoner of war) camp. This experience was very difficult, but its intense realism prepared the Marines for war. We soon began to realize that all this training was for real and that he would probably be called into action.

As the talk of war was upon the nation, the reality of Chris leaving for the Middle East set in. We went to the Miramar Base when the squadron and their families were being prepared. We felt reassured that the Marines would be taking good care of our loved ones, had trained them well, and would always be there for us. However, the suspense and secrecy as to when the squadron would be leaving made us quite nervous and put us on edge. The apprehension was growing, just thinking of our service people entering into a foreign area of the world, of starting an operation that was dividing the American people, and of the possible future threat to the United States.

Chris' e-mails and letters from Kuwait really helped give us a picture of his life and the flying missions that he and his pilot, Captain Rudy Rickner, were experiencing. Chris wrote,

> The war started three days ago, at least for my squadron it did. No one came into the ready room and said, "OK, we're at war." After a few hours of increased "up-tempo" requests for more sorties (flying missions), and guys coming back with empty bomb racks, we looked at each other and said, "Well, I guess this is it."

Chris's letters describing difficult night flying took our breath away. In one, he wrote:

> Last night's flight was difficult, to say the least. The clouds were solid from 5,000 feet to 30,000 feet. We were in the so-called "milk bowl" where you don't know which way is up or down. They taught us this in flight school, but I never imagined we would experience it the way we did last night.

I really didn't want to dwell on images like these, yet I could feel his excitement and sense of purpose.

> Last night we supported the ground troops in their advance to an objective. A most memorable flight that I would love to talk about at another time.

Alex, an elementary-school student in the neighborhood, gathered e-mails, pictures, and information about Chris's missions in Iraq and gave a presentation to his class. It was titled "My Hero." Alex wrote, "Sometimes when he flew over Iraq the enemy shot at him." Chris had written about some of their target areas being in the middle of a surface-to-air threat zone (AAA) and described them as looking like fireworks but much more lethal.

Children like Alex sent letters, packages, and drawings that Chris has saved to this day. The children wrote phrases like these: "We will pray for you," "Thanks for keeping our country safe," "Enclosed are Valentines for you and your fellow Marines," "My grandfather fought in WW II," " I love F/A-18s," and "Thanks for writing back to us and we are praying for peace."

My faith in Christ was the main source for strength, though there were still times when I was full of worry. Maybe I wasn't fully realizing what could happen to Chris. He was always handling situations well—he has leadership qualities and solves problems quickly. Yet there were times when I'd be in church and stay after, alone, crying, and wondering why no one else was feeling my pain. The rosary began to seem like a part of me, and saying the prayers seemed soothing. So there were moments of confidence that he would be okay and moments of uncertainty and anxiety. I am grateful for having a wonderful and sensitive husband. Talking and praying with Jim was and is a blessing, and I thank God for him and our children.

Chris and his fiancé were planning on being married in June of 2003. We weren't sure when the squadron would be finished with its mission in Iraq. This was very hard on the bride's family, but especially stressful for the future bride and groom. It was decided that they would go ahead with the plans and hope for the best. The squadron did return in time and they were married.

We were fortunate to be able to send and receive e-mails during

Chris's deployment. I have often thought about my grandmother, sending her two young sons off to World War II. Letters and photos were few and far between. Chris was able to send e-mails with photos during short breaks between planning and flying. We saw photos of his fourteen-man tent, of Chris flying in daylight, their tent headquarters, the dry, dusty surroundings, and his fellow Marines. Being able to picture in my mind his living and working environment helped me to understand what he was doing there.

Chris got his call sign, "Sparky," during his first deployment to the Pacific region. I heard that he was rather rambunctious and rowdy over there. I wonder what he was doing!

It was interesting to receive Chris's letters about the flights with his pilot, Captain Rudy Rickner. Chris, a WSO (Weapons Sensors Officer), was in the backseat, managing the weapons, sensors, navigation, and communications aboard the F/A-18D. They had trained together, so I know that they were fairly confident. Chris wrote, "We are doing well and seem to have a good understanding of what the other is doing and thinking."

I did feel that this was true, so I relaxed, keeping positive thoughts. But one evening when I was watching the news of the war (not a good activity if you had a loved one in a war!), I saw that an F/A-18 went down. I sat there trying to figure out if this was a dream or reality. Then I heard them describe the plane, and it was a single-seater. I was so relieved, but also shaken, and worried about the pilot who had gone down.

We encouraged family, neighbors, and friends to write letters and send pictures and articles from home. Chris wrote these thoughts in an article in the local paper:

> The other day I received a letter from my parents. In the envelope they included the front page of the *Plain Dealer* the day after the "Support the Troops" rally. I cannot begin to tell you how proud this made me feel. In the picture I saw people

> cheering in their winter hats and gloves. To those individuals at the rally, I would like to say: Seeing that picture and reading about the rally helps us over here in ways you can't imagine. Thank you. To all my family and friends in Chagrin Falls, thank you so much. I have received more support from you all via mail and e-mail than I could have asked for. I am proud to serve you all. Thank you, Cleveland.

I tried to send Chris a package that contained a rosary for him. I was told that no religious articles could be sent. I guess I made a scene in the post office—upset, tears running down my face, protesting the regulation. That was a day of anger for me. We were sending our loved ones into harm's way, but we couldn't send something that might bring them hope and comfort.

Discussions about the war in Iraq were at times quite uncomfortable. We had a son fighting in the war, and we had some family and friends who were against the war. We were guarded in our discussions and comments. Citizens in our country have freedom of speech and opinion, so we respected that principle. We learned to remain quiet and move on.

I think people realized that I had someone in the war whenever a military unit with American flags marched by in holiday parades, moving me to tears and sometimes uncontrollable crying. "Traveling Soldier," written by Bruce Robison and Farrah Braniff, and sung by the Dixie Chicks, tore my heart out! The words "Don't worry, I won't be able to write for a while" sounded familiar. Chris had e-mailed that we shouldn't worry if we didn't hear from him for a while because communication might be stopped. I guessed this meant that their missions had started. The traveling soldier that the Dixie Chicks were singing about did not come back. When I listen to that song, I always feel deeply for those affected by war.

Chris wrote,

> Despite the desert environment and living conditions, spirits are very high. It is amazing how one can be uprooted from everything they know and love, be put in an environment like this, and still be happy.

After reading comments like these, I would feel that things would be okay and that he had made a choice in life that he was not regretting.

Chris has just finished three years of teaching Navy ROTC at Vanderbilt University in Nashville, Tennessee. He will leave the Marines in September, after nine-and-a-half years of service. I feel that he will always stay connected to the Marines and service to his country in some way. The military training has been invaluable and the ties are strong. He will now take some time to decide what is next for him.

We have gained so much respect for our veterans and go out of our way to acknowledge their service and sacrifice. We love to hear their stories and hope that they are sharing them with their families and keeping their experiences alive.

As a watercolorist, I have been thinking about volunteer work with residents in nursing homes. Maybe it will be with the "Wounded Warriors." We'll see. We will be praying for peace in the world and for all people who are trying to bring about peace. My son, Captain C.T. "Sparky" Clark, flew thirty-five missions from February 1, 2003 to May 6, 2003.

Fran Clark married her husband, Jim, in 1963. They had three children, adopted a toddler, and then had one more child. Fran earned a master's degree in education and a master's in community counseling. For a while she had a small business selling antique wicker furniture; now she enjoys watercolor painting, volunteering, and being active in her church.

A Bond of Love

Connie Stephens-Gehri

THERE IS A SPECIAL bond between a mother and her son. When you're a single mother, that bond seems even tighter. When my first husband and I decided to end our marriage, I vowed I would do everything within my power to make life for our son, Derek, as enjoyable as possible. Working from my home gave me the opportunity to be involved in every aspect of Derek's life. We had weekly visits to the zoo, yearly passes to Geauga Lake, and campouts in the backyard. During Derek's' school years, I had the joy of being a room mother and a PTA mom. I never missed a soccer, baseball, or basketball game. Together, we were a mighty team of two; life was good.

As time went on, however, Derek grew up and became more and more his own person. Although I missed the time we spent with each other, he still made time for me, talking to me about many things his friends would never talk to their parents about. I shouldn't have been surprised at what he told me when he turned eighteen, in 2002. "Mom, I'm thinking about joining the National Guard." When those words left his mouth, I reacted the way any mother would and told him, "No way!" I was afraid.

I explained all of this to him and the subject was dropped. Six months later, just when I thought he'd finally seen my side, he enlisted. This time he told me after the fact. My son was a man, and had made a manly decision. God, in his wisdom, was not going to let me walk this road alone. Somewhere between Derek signing the papers and shipping off to boot camp, I met the man who would become my husband. He would also become my support and shoulder to cry on.

Derek's first deployment was in July of 2004, to Kosovo. I remember clearly the day he left. I didn't want to let go of this six-foot-four-inch young man who I could still clearly see as a happy twelve-year-old child. He looked down at me and said, "We won't say goodbye, we'll just say—see you later." I was stoic until the bus pulled away, and then I sobbed.

Once there, Derek was able to phone me. On a weekly basis, we'd exchange e-mail, letters, and cards and talk on the phone. At first, as he was adjusting to being so far from everything he loved, we talked frequently. As he became accustomed to life on base, the calls slowed down. He was getting used to his new adventure.

Then he injured his knee and phoned to say they were flying him to Germany for surgery. I couldn't get there and spent agonizing hours waiting for the doctor's call. I felt helpless. Eventually, after some long talks with Army superiors, it was decided Derek would come home. What a homecoming that was. My son was home and I was as happy as any mother would be.

In 2007, word came of a new deployment. I was sick. Would this mean Iraq? I joked with friends that if that were the case, I would sneak into his room while he was asleep and break his other knee if it meant keeping him home. Although I wouldn't have, the crazy and desperate thought did enter my grieving mind for a moment. Finally, the news arrived that he'd be going to Kuwait. He would train at Fort Hood, Texas, for a few months then deploy to Kuwait. Derek would be gone for over a year. Perhaps because he was older and close to finishing his criminal justice degree, I wasn't as worried until the moment came for the second "see you later." He practically had to peel me off of him.

At the beginning, I would spot a car that looked like his and for a split second my heart would leap for joy, only to be reminded of the reality of things. I surrounded myself with pictures of his going-away party and cherished each and every e-mail he sent to me. The first one is my particular favorite.

> Hey mom, I'm here in Kuwait, it's hot as nuts here! I'm living in a shitty tent for 8 days till everyone else gets here. The base is nice, palm trees line the divided streets that run in the middle of the base. It kind of sucks though, cause the dust is everywhere here. I made it though and will make the best out of it here. If you could send some Crocs shoes size 12, we need them for the showers since there are scorpions here. I will send you a list of some of the other things I will need.
> I miss you.
> Luv ya, Derek

Technology has made this separation much more bearable. We both have webcams and speakers on our computers, something I wasn't too sure I wanted. Seeing him for the first time on the webcam, I had tears of joy and sadness. We made faces at each other and laughed; it was wonderful. He looked good, but too skinny. Long work hours and 120-degree heat have resulted in thirty-five lost pounds. I send goodie boxes often, filled with his favorite snacks and magazines and silly little toys, and always include a picture of our golden retriever dressed up in Derek's clothes, to make him laugh. I even created a MySpace page so we can both download pictures faster.

As I write this, Derek has already served six months with another six months to go. He works in security at the front gate and finally admitted to me that he's found several car bombs on his detail. He was so proud to tell me, and he was commended by his superiors for doing such a great job. I am proud, but my heart skips a beat each time I think of him. In less than a month, he gets to come home for a twelve-day leave. I look forward to holding on to him but not to saying "see you later."

Connie Stephens-Gehri was a hair designer for more than thirty years and is now semi-retired. She and her husband keep busy with six granddaughters. She loves to recycle antiques and used items into unique arts and crafts she sells at juried shows throughout the year. She does volunteer work and helps the USO and her son's National Guard Family Readiness Group.

Essay for Sam

Marilyn Benjamin

MY SON, SAM, WAS a Gulf War vet who died in 2005 at age thirty-four while working as a defense contractor, not in Iraq, but in South Korea. He was in the field artillery and was sent to fight in Desert Storm at age twenty. Each time I pick up the newspaper and read about someone's son being killed or injured, or just see photos of someone's son going off to war, it brings back those days and a flood of emotions.

My son had been in the Army since age eighteen. The military always held a fascination for him and as soon as he was old enough, he enlisted. When we went to see him graduate from basic training, his sergeant said that when he first looked at Sam he wasn't sure he would make it, but my son wanted it so badly that he proved him wrong. My son never held his head as high as when he wore that uniform. It gave him the structure, the camaraderie, and the confidence he needed to grow into a man. I was so proud.

When his unit was deployed, I think it seemed surreal to both of us. Everything that was taught in theory or played in war games now was to become real. It is hard to describe what it felt like to send a son to war. It was against every instinct I had as a mother. A mother's job is to keep her children safe; as a child I warned him not to chase a ball into the street, to wear his jacket so he wouldn't catch a cold, not to play with matches. And now I was to willingly send my child off into the gravest of danger.

After he left, I remember packing boxes for him almost every day. It became my therapy to pack a box to ship to him: cookies, magazines, grooming items, items that he asked for, like warm gloves, hand warmers (knowing that by the time he got them it would be summer again in the desert), pictures from home. All the while I was feeling like my son was on the railroad tracks with a train fast approaching. I needed to snatch him from harm's way, but all I could do was bake cookies! The Gulf War was the first war we could watch in real time on TV, and I was glued to the TV, in terror and in hope. Every shred of information sustained me. I felt like part of me was there with him. If I knew where he was, maybe just my knowing would protect him. In support of the troops during the Gulf War, there were flags lining the streets. As I drove anywhere, I felt like our soldiers' efforts were being appreciated. I found comfort in those American flags, as though the nation's collective thoughts could protect him.

It was a short war, thank God. I don't know how I would have sustained the stress of knowing he was in battle any longer. I cannot imagine how the families cope with the length of the current conflict. After the war, my son was in Kuwait for months, guarding the oil wells that Saddam Hussein had set on fire. He described the smell and the black soot that coated everything he was wearing, and even got into his nostrils. I was concerned about long-term health effects of breathing that polluted air.

When he finally came home, he returned to Austin, where his base was, and stayed there even after he was discharged. The long-term effects turned out to be mostly emotional. He tried to get on with his life, but he suffered from nightmares and depression. He told his sisters (not me) that he saw (and probably did) terrible things while liberating Kuwait. He told them about prisoners left tied up in the desert (he wondered if anyone ever came for them or if they suffered terrible deaths), children killed and maimed while being used as shields by the Iraqi forces, and things he said he couldn't talk about. He had some short-term VA counseling and I hoped he would feel better soon. He did not. Eventually, he re-enlisted. He said no one would ever understand war except another soldier and he wanted to surround himself again with soldiers. He said life had changed for him. His family were now his friends and his friends (fellow soldiers) were now his family.

Later, he was sent to South Korea and was stationed there for almost eight years. The Army was his life, but he had an opportunity to work for a defense contracting firm that provided computerized battle training to the Army, and he took the job when his tour of duty was over. It seemed like the best of all worlds to him, still doing military training, but seemingly without the risk. Safe at last, I thought.

Then I got the phone call every parent dreads. My son had been attacked and beaten coming out of a bar by some South Korean thugs and suffered massive internal injuries. He had emergency surgery in Korea, and they weren't sure he would live. His stepfather and I went to Korea, possibly to see him for the last time. While in Korea, we witnessed protests against the American military presence. Navigating around a demonstration one day, an elderly cab driver apologized to us, saying that the protesters were young and they didn't appreciate how much Americans helped during the Korean War.

With my son gravely injured, I remember resenting those demonstrations, and just wanting to get him back to the United States. After a month in a Korean hospital, suffering complication after complication, my son was finally able to be flown home by air ambulance, and then he was in and out of hospitals here, until he lost his final battle. I remember, though, when he arrived from Korea and was being admitted to the hospital in Cleveland, his first comments were that the bed was so comfortable and everything was so clean. Even though he was not killed in action, he was a veteran and we gave him a military funeral. Maybe not as heroic a death as some, but he served his country, and I think he would have appreciated it. I know the ceremony and the presence of soldiers there were a comfort to me.

Life for me is forever changed. I am now the one with the dreams and the depression. I see him in every young man I see in uniform. I privately grieve each injury and each loss I read about in the paper or see on the news. I ache for each mother who knows the pain of that loss. It has been seventeen years since my son served in the Gulf War, and I pray that this war ends soon. I pray that the men and women who vote to send our children into danger, whether it be in Korea, or Iraq, or Afghanistan, understand the magnitude of this sacrifice . . . leaving a country where things are so comfortable and so clean to serve in countries where our presence may or may not even be appreciated.

Marilyn Benjamin is a registered nurse. Sam was the third of her four children, and her only son.

Marine Flag Flying

Kara Paine

IT IS HARD TO describe the feelings you have being the mother of someone in the U.S. military. While I am the proudest a mom could possibly be, I am also scared out of my mind. Prayer has taken on a whole new meaning.

My son is a corporal in the U.S. Marines. After high school graduation, he attended Kent State University for two years. He came home in March of his second year and told us he wanted to join the Marines. Two days after returning to school, he called and said, "I've gone to Cleveland and taken the oath."

He served one tour of duty in Iraq, and is currently serving his second in Afghanistan. He feels that things are worse in Afghanistan, but we don't really know what he is going through. We hear bits and pieces in letters, and in very few phone calls, but he isn't allowed to reveal much information. He's said, "Things are bad, and conditions are worse."

In Iraq, he served with a military police unit. They drove convoys part of the time, looking for IEDs, set up roadblocks, and did search and patrol the rest of the time. They were out five to seven days at a time, then back to the FOB (forward operating base).

In Afghanistan he is with an operations unit doing fire direction control. His unit was out five weeks and supposed to go back to the FOB, but orders were changed, and they spent another five weeks out. This happened several times, and his unit ended up being out three-and-a-half months.

Of course there were no showers during that time because their water supply is low. They wash clothes in artillery casings, using bottled water. I can't begin to imagine how miserable it is for our guys in the desert heat, wearing full gear, on limited sleep, and not being able to bathe. America as a whole has no idea what they are going through, and what they deal with day in and day out.

While he was in Iraq, he lost one of his best friends. They had only been there three weeks and were out on patrol, driving armored Humvees. His friend, a gunner, was hit by enemy fire. My son was in a different vehicle but heard the call over the radio and had the sickening feeling it was his friend who had been hit.

During his second month in Iraq, he was injured. He was on patrol again, driving a Humvee. The vehicle in front of him hit a roadside bomb, and the back of it was blown up. Believe it or not, no one in that vehicle was injured. However, the impact of the explosion blew the tires out on my son's vehicle and forced him off the road. To be honest, I don't think he really knows what happened. He said, "I remember seeing a flash and came to hours later in a daze, aware that something had happened. I was unable to see or hear. "

He was flown out of the area in a medevac helicopter and to a hospital on the base. He had a serious concussion and a fractured eye socket, which required surgery, and permanently lost partial vision in one eye and hearing in one ear. My soldier also had several broken ribs.

He said, "My eye looks like a black-and blue-baseball, stitching and all." He was in the hospital for thirteen days. He called and told us he had been in an explosion and had a bad concussion, and that he was sending a letter to explain everything. We knew he didn't sound right on the phone, but we had no idea how serious things were until we received his letter.

He did not get to come home. They patched him up and sent him right back to active duty. A week after that, the father of his girlfriend of five years passed away from cancer. My son was very close to him, having worked with, and ridden to and from work with him for three summers, and during school vacations. He was like a second father to my son, and dealing with his death was very hard. It was a tremendous loss for my son.

Of course being in Iraq, there was nothing he could do. He talked to every officer he could and tried to come home but was denied because it was not an immediate family member. At the end of that same month, he also lost a grandfather to cancer and was not allowed to come home for that, either.

During all of this, he also lost his girlfriend. She just stopped writing to him and quit answering his phone calls. I think the death of her father was too much for her to handle. The hardest thing for me was not being able to put my arms around him and tell him things would be okay.

There are days, weeks, and months that we don't hear from our soldier. I have that constant fear in the back of my mind that something has happened.

During his first deployment he was gone during Halloween. We have a Marine flag flying on the front porch and live in a very small town. Some Halloween pranksters decided to turn it upside down on the flagpole. We didn't notice, but a former Marine did. He thought that either something happened, or we were mad and being disrespectful to the Corps. He called the police station to have them check on it.

A policeman showed up at our house around 8 P.M. No one ever uses our front door—everyone goes to the back. Of course, I was the only one home at the time. I can't even describe my fear when I opened the door and saw the policeman standing there. My first thought was that something had happened to my son, and he was there to tell me, even though I knew a Marine would come if something had happened. Explaining about the flag, the policeman asked, "Did something happen to your son?" I was so embarrassed, and fixed the flag immediately.

I have come home from work or grocery shopping countless times and driven around the block, afraid to pull up in front of the house for fear that a car will be sitting there, waiting to give me bad news. In our family, I have always been the strong one, and not one to worry, but sometimes fear takes hold of you. It has this powerful grip that won't let go.

When my son left for Iraq, I wished that a small piece of the boy who left would remain in the man who returned. During the first two months of that deployment, he changed from a boy into a man. When he was home on leave, he slept on the couch, not in his bed. As I watched him sleep and dream, I saw expressions on his face I had never seen before. He has many haunting memories. He has shared some of the things that happened and things he lived through, but I am sure not all.

My son was supposed to come home at the end of September, but his time has been extended to mid-November. I am anxiously awaiting his return. My heart goes out to every family that has a son, daughter, niece, nephew, father, or mother serving our country. I have the utmost respect for all of them.

Kara Paine works in a veterinary clinic as a receptionist. She and her husband, Harold, have three children.

One Day at a Time

Marcy Redmond

IT WAS A HOT summer day in August 2005 when I drove my son Sheridan to the recruiting office in Lakewood, Ohio. He had joined the Army to become part of the military police and travel the world. I thought this was the most difficult day of my life. I wasn't prepared to say goodbye to my son. Not this way. You see, it's not the same as when your son or daughter goes to college. With the military, you lose the freedom to call your child whenever you want. He belongs to the Army now. I just wasn't ready for this. But what choice did I have? I had to learn how to become a military mom. I felt so alone in my world. None of my friends were going through this. I knew I had to find other mothers like me. So I contacted the USO to see if they knew about a mothers' support group. They did. I joined the Mothers of Military (M.O.M.). It was the best thing I could have done. The support has been wonderful.

Now, the next step was to make it through basic training. Sheridan's basic training was at Fort Leonard Wood, Missouri. I waited every weekend for his two- to three-minute call. It always ended with "I've got to go. Someone else needs the phone. Love you, Mom."

Finally graduation day came on February 16, 2006. My husband, Ed, and my son, Patrick, and I flew to Missouri to share this wonderful day with Sheridan. I would not have missed this day for anything. I was so very proud of him. Afterward, we all drove to the airport together. Sheridan flew home separately, but we would all be home again within hours.

After his leave, Sheridan went on to Germany. It was now March of 2006. Saying goodbye hadn't gotten any easier. The future scared me so. I knew Germany meant more intense training, preparing my soldier for Iraq. I wasn't going to think about that for now. I hoped that he would have off-duty time to explore Germany. And he did. His e-mail read:

> Hey Mom, this weekend I went to Leipzig, Germany to visit my friends Dan, Jack, and Sara. We spent the first night hanging out with everyone and going to two bars and this town square where they have a 50 ft by 50 ft TV playing soccer games. On Saturday we went to a petting zoo then the Leipzig zoo. We had a lot of fun. Sunday we had some good brunch and said our goodbyes. I have to go to work. Bye Mom.

It warmed my heart to know he was accomplishing his dream of traveling. As for his military training he wrote,

> I'm doing some good training and enjoying my time greatly right now. I hope everything is fine back home. Give my regards to everyone. Love you Mom.

When October 2006 rolled around Sheridan informed me he was coming home for a two-week leave. I didn't understand why he'd give up the opportunity to see Europe, using this time to travel. Finally, after I asked him why one time too many, he explained to me the real reason he was coming home. He wrote,

I will see the world. I have plenty of time to do that but coming home in October is more important.

He was going to be deployed to Iraq.

I knew this day would come, but that didn't make it any easier. I just knew this homecoming had to be the best time for him—carefree and fun. We had a big party in his honor. All our family and friends came. I wanted Sheridan to know just how much everyone loved him.

All of our goodbyes have been very difficult for me. I cry easily, but this time was different. I prayed and prayed that God would give me the strength to not fall apart while we sat at the airport. He heard my prayers. I had to be strong for Sheridan. We hugged him and wished him well, not knowing what the future would hold. I miss him so.

The 127th Military Police Company did their patrols up and down the roads in Iraq, over and over again. Then on May 11, 2007, my husband and I were in our backyard. The phone rang. My husband answered the phone in the garage. He was not talking much, mostly listening to the caller. The caller was from the Army. Ed came over to me and told me that Sheridan's Humvee was hit by an IED. He was okay, with minor injuries. Nonetheless, I fell apart.

Now, the Army has entered my home. The shock was so great that it took me a while to realize how lucky Sheridan was and how thankful I was that he was alive. The best thing was hearing his voice when he called. I needed that call. There were three soldiers in the Humvee. Only two were lucky that day. Sheridan e-mailed his father about the incident:

Basically what happened that day was we were doing our normal everyday thing. We were the lead vehicle. I was the gunner. I was standing up and looking over to my left, I saw

> the box that had the four IED's in it. I started to think "o shit" but only got to the "o" then it went off. We then veered off into a ten-foot sewage ditch. After that it was a whole lot of pulling security and getting Farrar into a chopper. He died in-flight. The kid was only 126 pounds, with all of his injuries he didn't have a chance.

I will never forget that day or the loss of Specialist Tony Farrar Jr., a courageous and honorable soldier. He was Sheridan's good friend.

Sheridan's tour in Iraq was to be fifteen months. So now, we just wait until it's over. Sheridan's e-mails have become shorter and less frequent. A mother has to be patient and understand that the events a soldier goes through will change his life forever. All we can do is love them and pray that they come home healthy in body and mind.

It is now January 2008. He will be coming home soon. His tour in Iraq will be over by the end of January. Sheridan will be home for a one-month leave. I'm so excited. Now all I have to do is wait for the e-mail from the Family Readiness Group in Germany that the 127th Military Police Company is in the air.

This hasn't been easy. Because of Sheridan's choice in life, I have met and made some wonderful friends by joining two support groups, Blue Star Mothers of America and M.O.M. My life has also changed, and for the better. I thank Sheridan for what he has given me. I am so very proud of him. My message to military mothers is to just take one day at a time and you will survive being a military mom.

Marcy Redmond manages an animal hospital. She and her husband, Ed, have two sons. Marcy and Ed enjoy antiquing and going to flea markets whenever they have the chance. Marcy relaxes by tending to her perennial garden each spring and summer.

Frantic with Love

Kathy Leopold

THE BUMPER STICKER READS—MARINE MOM: TOUGHEST JOB IN THE CORPS. There is no doubt about that! My journey as a military mom started when we floated out of the recruiter's office. I was so proud of Jeff. A Marine—the best of the best! Little did I know how he would fight the initial breaking down and rebuilding process.

In hindsight, I should have seen the rough times ahead when Jeff refused to put on nice clothes the day recruiters came to get him. What a journey I was in for! Letters from boot camp were horrendous. They were so heartbreaking to read, but he passed the Crucible (the final test) and we attended a glorious graduation. School of Infantry (SOI) was challenging also, as I am sure it was supposed to be. The letters and calls were equally tough to read or listen to. Jeff was struggling to get through the physical and psychological experience of becoming a Marine. I knew this was a hard time for Jeff, but one he would hopefully look back on and smile. In my heart I knew he would survive. Nevertheless, I cried a lot and prayed that something would happen to make Jeff see the light. And it did.

One day Jeff called and said he had met a girl—a Marine. The next day he told me about getting in trouble for crossing the street without permission so he could talk with this girl. The third day he said the girl was no longer in the picture. After that incident, Jeff's attitude changed. He was more open to whatever was thrown his way. I chose to believe this girl was a guardian angel who said, "Jeff, get your Marine butt in gear!" and was then gone.

He finished SOI without any problems and was assigned to Marine Corps Base Hawaii. I couldn't believe after all he put himself through, Jeff was going to such a sought-after home base. Little did I know that his battalion—America's Battalion—would be deployed within seven months.

Now it really sank in that I would have a son going off to war. Never in my wildest dreams had I ever thought this could or would happen. I was proud and devastated at the same time: proud because Jeff was a well-trained Marine and devastated because I knew he would be going to those places that were on the news—all those killing places. Even though I had made it through so much already, my journey was about to continue down new paths that would test my courage and inner strength.

Right away, I wanted to know how I could help the troops. This led me to the USO. What a great find! I made it a point to volunteer for as many USO activities as I could: from Bob Hope golf outings to handing out USO information at a Cleveland Browns game, to selling USO care packages at a free Lee Greenwood concert, to collecting Christmas gifts for children of our local military. I have made the USO a part of my life.

Mothers of Military (M.O.M.), an offshoot of the USO in Northeast Ohio, has also been a great help in teaching me how to cope with having a son in Iraq. Almost all the moms who attend this support group have a son or daughter in Iraq or Afghanistan. At M.O.M. meetings we laugh and cry together, open our hearts to each other with unconditional love, share fears and joys, and ask those hard questions about what happens next. We encourage each other when those letters or calls from the front are real downers. I would not have been able to get through Jeff's first deployment without these new sisters.

While Jeff was on his first tour, I realized that many citizens from my town did not know that so many young men and women from Avon Lake were serving in the armed forces. As I talked with friends, they told me of someone they knew who was in the service, and I started to make a list. Pretty soon, people were calling me or stopping me on the street with another name for my list. The list now has grown to almost fifty names. Each year Jeff is in the Marines, I update the addresses on my list.

Military parents are so proud of their son or daughter. They are very happy to talk with another military parent in the same situation. I am so blessed to have these new friends who understand exactly how I feel. Many groups have asked for a copy of my list so they can send cards and packages to those presently serving in war zones. Church groups, school kids, tae kwon do classes, and even individual families have requested a copy of the list so they can send something to the troops. It is my privilege to be able to provide this information.

Do you have a Blue Star banner hanging in your window? I do. My love for Jeff and desire to support him have led me on a personal crusade to make sure each military family in Avon Lake has a Blue Star banner hanging in their window. All citizens need to know our children are putting their lives on the line for them 24/7. When our local VFW post (no. 8796) heard about my efforts to secure Blue Star banners, they contacted me and offered me a thousand dollars for Blue Star banners! I was blown away by their generosity. When I get a request, a free Blue Star banner is proudly hand-delivered. How satisfying it is to see the pride and joy on the mom's and dad's faces. How wonderful that a local organization came through to support its legacy!

My roller-coaster ride through the blasts of all these emotional ups and downs has been sustained by my faith in God. Recently, I received a email from God—isn't the Internet wonderful? He wrote, "This is God. Today I will be handling all of your problems for you. I love you. Have a nice day. God." So, that is exactly what I have been trying to do. All my worries go into the SFGTD (something for God to do) box, and I know they will be resolved in his time, not mine.

Through all this, the only change in my daily routine was that Jeff was *constantly* on my mind. Oh, yes—and more frequent trips to the post office to send letters and packages to Iraq. Luckily, America's Battalion's first deployment, from March to October of 2006, was very uneventful, from a mom's point of view. When Jeff called and complained that he was bored, I was so thankful for his boredom! The second deployment, July 2007 to February 2008, seemed much longer to me. I guess having been through the experience once made me more impatient to have Jeff back on American soil.

By the end of his second deployment, I had a new fear: post-traumatic stress disorder (PTSD). In phone calls from the front, I heard a great amount of stress in Jeff's voice. How should this Marine mom prepare to welcome home a son who may return with PTSD problems? How would these potential problems manifest themselves? Should I offer to help or should I just step back and let my little boy who was now a man work things out for himself? I was reminded of a poem that was given to me by an Army mom. One verse reads:

I am a caring mother
My son has gone to war . . .
My mind is filled with worries
That I have never known before
Every day I try to keep
My thoughts from turning black

I may be scared, but I am proud,
My son has got your back.

Yes, this mom was scared, but so proud that her son had served two successful tours of duty in Iraq, so proud that he had my back. I would continue to have his back when he was discharged and a civilian.

The journey is not over now that Jeff is home in the good old U.S. of A. Even though the tension and anger in his voice has been replaced by calm and easiness, there is still the future to think about. It makes this Marine mom happy to hear that the "seniors" (those whose time in the Corps is almost completed) are being readied for life after the military. TAP (Transitions Assistance Program) classes are helping the young men and women cope with the changes needed to make the transition to civilian life. And there are no signs of PTSD—yet. Jeff sounds better each time I get to talk with him. As his spirits rise, so do mine.

My journey as a military mom taught me to "let go and let God." It taught me to cope with the fact that Jeff was in harm's way. I am confident that I will be able to cope with whatever personal baggage Jeff brought home from Iraq. I am so proud that my Jeff is a Marine. Sometimes, I just start crying. And sometimes I am just frantic with love!

Kathy Leopold is retired from teaching physical education and coaching various sports, but she still works as a substitute teacher. She and her husband adopted two boys. Kathy enjoys quilting (she has won blue ribbons at the county fair), reading, and travel.

My Story

Ilena Porter

WE LEFT OHIO AND drove all night to Jacksonville, North Carolina, that October day in 2005. My oldest son, Jack, drove and Tony, my youngest son and our Marine, rode up front with him. The two of them laughed and talked all the way down, reminiscing about all the things they did when they were kids. I pretended to sleep, but I was listening to every word and every story they were telling. While listening to them, it was all I could do to keep from crying. I am so proud of my sons and what they have accomplished in their lives. I had a big lump in my throat and tears in my eyes, but I knew I had to be strong and hold on. I knew I couldn't break down and let them know how I really felt about Tony leaving for Iraq.

When Tony was young he would always tell people when he grew up he wanted to be an Army guy. But as Tony got older, he discovered there were different branches of service and that what he really wanted to be was a Marine. It came as no surprise when Tony joined the Marine Corps his senior year of high school. I would have probably felt a little better about him joining if it wasn't during a time of war. But I knew that was what he wanted to do. I knew I had to support him.

Tony left for Parris Island on September 19, 2004. While he was in boot camp, he wrote me every week. I looked forward to getting those letters from him. They always seemed to come on Thursday, and I would always hurry home from work so I could get to the post office and get his letter. Tony graduated from boot camp on December 14, 2004, and we traveled to Parris Island for his graduation. My husband, Dan, who was Tony's stepfather, was really excited about returning to Parris Island to see how much it had changed since he graduated in 1972.

The day before graduation is Family Day. Tony took us on a tour and showed us all around the base. Then he took us to his barracks. Dan said, "Open that footlocker and let me see how it looks." When Tony opened his footlocker there was a letter taped inside the lid that Dan had sent him. Tony told him, "That letter was my motivation and helped me make it through boot camp. Anytime I felt like quitting or giving up, I would read that letter and push on."

After Tony's graduation from boot camp he went to Camp Geiger in North Carolina for his MCT (Marine Combat Training) course. Upon completion of the course, he was sent to Pensacola, Florida, to begin his MOS (military occupational specialty) training. Tony was there for approximately four months and then was sent to Camp Johnson in Jacksonville, North Carolina. Upon completion of school at Camp Johnson, he was assigned to his permanent duty station, New River Air Station in Jacksonville, North Carolina.

Tony came home on leave in July 2005, and shortly after he returned to North Carolina, he called and told me he had volunteered to deploy to Iraq. I asked him, "Why?"

He said, "That is something I wanted to do." I was feeling all kinds of emotions when he told me this. I was proud, scared, and wanted to tell him he was crazy and what was he thinking, wanting to go off to war.

It brought back memories of when I was twelve years old. My uncle left for Vietnam because he wanted to go, and he didn't make it back. He was killed in the line of duty in 1969. I will never forget that Saturday morning while we were eating breakfast. A taxi pulled up in front of our house. My grandmother went to the door, and when she saw the man coming up to the door she knew why he was there. She just fell into her chair beside the door and refused to answer it. My dad went to the door and took the telegram.

Was that going to happen to me too? How would I deal with that? What should I do or say to talk him out of going? I knew he was a young man now, and it was his decision, not mine. I had to be strong and support him.

A few months passed and before we knew it, it was October, the month I didn't want to come—the month he was due to deploy. Tony drove his car back to Ohio because he wanted his brother to take care of it while he was gone. While he was home, Tony spent some time with his father, who had a lot of medical problems at the time. When Tony's leave was up, Jack, Dan, and I drove him back to North Carolina.

After arriving at our motel in North Carolina, Tony called the base to let them know he was back. We all went out for an early dinner. I just couldn't eat due to that lump in my throat getting bigger and bigger, and knowing the time was getting closer and this would be our last night together before he left. While we were at the restaurant everyone kept asking me, "Aren't you going to eat more than that?" All I could say was, "Maybe I'll get something later."

On the drive back to the motel, I lost it. I tried so hard not to, but I started to cry and couldn't stop. Tony asked me, "What's wrong?" I told him, "I don't want you to go to Iraq!" He kept assuring me everything was going to be okay and he'd be back before we knew it.

Suddenly, Tony got a call that he needed to report back to the base ASAP. There was a change in plans and he would be leaving that night. We drove him to the base and he finished his last-minute packing. I'd made up a box with cookies, brownies, and a couple of jars of my homemade pepper butter to take along. Tony stuffed the goodies in one of his bags and said, "Mom, quit worrying. Everything is going to be okay."

Before we knew it, the bus pulled in. After all the gear was loaded and the Marines got on the bus, it pulled away. I told Jack to follow the bus as long as he could off the base. I wanted to keep it in my sight. I don't know why I wanted to follow that bus, but it just made me feel better having it in my sight. Our drive back to the motel was a long, quiet one. I don't think any of us said anything to each other.

Tony went to Iraq aboard a Navy ship, the USS *Nassau*, with the 22nd Marine Expeditionary Unit. He called from the ship and sent me e-mails while he was making his way across the Atlantic. They stopped at a few ports in Europe before they got to Kuwait.

The first couple of months of Tony's deployment were an emotional roller coaster for me. I started a new job, my mother had a stroke, my sons' father was dying, and my son was on his way to Iraq. I never felt as alone in my whole life as I did then. I couldn't sleep. My eyes were always bloodshot and full of tears. I always had that big lump in my throat.

It was really hard trying to stay focused at work. People would constantly ask me, "Have you heard from Tony?" "Aren't you scared that he's over there?" "Did you hear on the news that there were some Marines killed?" I just wanted to scream, "Well what the hell do you think? How would you feel? Guess what, I watch the news all the time, and yeah, I know some Marines were killed!"

I know people didn't do it intentionally. They were just asking. There is one girl at work who would stop by and see me a lot. She too was a mother of two Marines who had served in Iraq, so she truly knew exactly how I felt and what I was going through.

Tony was flown home on emergency leave from Kuwait to be with his father before he passed away. Tony arrived home on December 24, 2005, and his father passed away on December 27. Tony had to go back to Iraq on January 5. His unit had already left Kuwait and flown into Anbar province in Iraq. Tony had to make the flight alone into Iraq without his unit. My husband, Dan, being a former Marine, said that had to have been very difficult for Tony because the Marines are like a band of brothers and are always there for each other.

My mother passed away on January 12, 2006. I contacted the Red Cross and asked them if a chaplain could deliver the message to Tony, whose father had passed away just sixteen days earlier, on his last visit home. Tony called home later that night and told me he took the message from the Red Cross. Taking and delivering messages was one of his duties.

The next few months went by very slowly. Every payday, I would go shopping for a care package to send to Tony. I got a new puppy Tony helped me name via e-mails. Finally, April arrived and that meant one thing: Tony would be home in a month.

April seemed like it had sixty days instead of thirty. Before we knew it, it was May and we were on our way to North Carolina for the homecoming. It was one of the most awesome and emotional things I ever experienced.

I made sure we were all up early and one of the first families to arrive at the base. We got there between 7:30 and 8:00 A.M. The day was beautiful, warm—in the seventies. Driving to the base from the motel we saw signs posted everywhere saying WELCOME HOME, WE MISSED YOU!

Finally, we were standing in the crowd at the base waiting for the helicopters to fly in with our Marines aboard. The helicopters flew over the top of the crowd of loved ones—children, mothers, fathers, brother, sisters, husbands, and wives. The crowd was cheering, waving their flags and waiting for the helicopters to land so we could embrace our Marines.

I overheard one of the wives talking about her husband. "I hope I can find him," she said. I knew I was not going to have any problems finding Tony. He told me he would be flying in on the last helicopter and would be proudly carrying the guidon (the colors) for his unit.

The Marines, in formation, started to march across the landing strip. There he was—my son. He was right up front, proudly carrying the guidon. When they started marching across the pavement, everyone just went running. I ran toward Tony and just kept calling his name until I finally got his attention. Tony seemed so different, so grown up. When he left he was my nineteen-year-old son, my baby. He came back a twenty-year-old young man.

This is my story of my son's first deployment to Iraq. It took me three days to write this, as I cried a lot trying to put this together. I look back and ask myself, "How did I make it through that deployment?" The only answer I have is prayer, lots and lots of prayers. As I write this story, Tony is currently on his second deployment.

Ilena Porter works full time as a secretary at a prison and enjoys a very simple, rural life. She has two sons, a stepson, a stepdaughter, and eight step-grandchildren. She likes to bake and make quilts for family and friends; she has entered pies, cakes, and cookies and a few quilts over the years at her local county fair, winning numerous ribbons.

Nothing Prepares You

Marian Murawski

I THOUGHT I WAS PREPARED for our son's deployment (January–October 2005). I was a Key Volunteer for our son's Marine battalion. I purposely took the training course three times so I would be prepared. A Key Volunteer for the Marine Corps is a liaison between the military and the families. A KV relays messages from the command to the families, helps solve problems the families may encounter, and sometimes just listens to family members when they need someone to listen.

I attended everything the Marine Corps had to offer the families—an information day about what to expect during deployment and what help is available, Family Days (picnics with information about the Marines), and an information day about what to expect when our Marines came home.

I attended KV meetings every month, but all of that training and information went out the window when my son's unit suffered a large number of casualties and we didn't hear from Jim for days after that. I forgot that if he were injured severely, we would be notified. I remembered we would receive a visit if the worst happened, but forgot that it wouldn't be after the deaths were announced in the news.

Many days later, I finally received a phone call. I immediately burst into tears and told Jim, "I am so happy to hear from you." Jim's reply was "Mom, you know I'm not stationed there." He was a cook, but I knew that he rode in convoys and I wasn't sure where he ended up in those convoys and what he would have to do when he got there. He later received a Navy commendation (presented for sustained acts of heroism or meritorious service) in part because he was involved in so many convoys. When Jim came home, he showed all of us a video of an IED exploding during a convoy, very close to his vehicle. No one was injured—the IED was buried wrong.

My girlfriend told me her nephews enlisted in the military. I cried. My niece's boyfriend enlisted. I cried. I couldn't figure out why I cried until my sister pointed out that I know what the moms will go through. *Nothing* prepares you.

Marian Murawski grew up in the Vietnam era and always hoped her children would not have wars in their lifetime. She is currently a housewife (she tells people she is a "domestic goddess") and fills her time sewing, doing various crafts, volunteering, and helping others. She cherishes the rare times when her whole family is together—including the pets!

I Love You—Please Remember to Pray

Lucky Caswell Harris

ARE WE EVER REALLY prepared for our children to leave home to go to college, get married, or begin employment? What do we say when our child decides to take a big step in life and doesn't ask, "Mother, may I?" How do we let our "babies" go to make choices on their own? What if we don't understand the choice they have made?

When Meka, the younger of my two daughters, informed me that she had joined the Army, I became instantly ill. (Thank God, I was already lying in bed!) I hoped that she was playing one of her infamous jokes, but after I regained my composure, I realized it was no joke. The words "Mom, I joined the Army" kept replaying in slow motion in my brain, like molasses seeping through my nerves. Meka waited for my reaction as she placed the Army T-shirt and video on my bed. I was at once bombarded with feelings of fear, anger, and pride. I took a deep breath, and as I looked at her standing at the foot of my bed, our short life as mother and daughter flashed across a high-definition screen in my mind. What an honor I felt to have birthed this woman-child! As these

thoughts drifted in and out of my consciousness, I knew that what I said at that moment would make a world of difference in the days, months, and years to come.

"Lucky, stop," I said to myself. "God, dear God, give me the strength to speak, give me the right words to say!" I sat up and smiled at her, and with the strongest voice I could muster said, "I love you. Are you sure this is what you want to do?"

"Yes."

"Why?!" I wanted but did not dare to scream out loud. Instead, I simply responded, "I am so proud of you. You know that whatever you do or need, I support you and will always be there for you." Her face and body relaxed, and we hugged one another as I whispered, "I love you . . . please, always remember to pray."

Now, if I thought that moment was difficult, well, let me tell you, compared to the following years, that lesson in fear, faith, and fortitude was a cakewalk! As we traveled the journey of a military family, I maintained my sanity with another alliterative phrase: patience, prayer, and promise. Meka joined the Army in 2000 and was deployed for her entire tour of duty. How do we watch as our children leave for war? There are so many questions, and no clear answers. Not hearing from Meka for days, sometimes months, was downright frightening. As mothers, we always think we have control—even when we lose it. We want to maintain control. Losing this control is not easy! And so we pray.

After missed phone calls, hundreds of prayers, care packages, the terror of 9/11, and holidays and family gatherings without Meka at our table, we finally made it through four years of deployments. And yes, we remembered to pray: a prayer of thanksgiving!

Just when I thought I could exhale, Meka informed me that she had joined the National Guard to fulfill her remaining obligations to the military! Once again, those same feelings from four years earlier resurfaced.

The National Guard? Would that mean that she could stay home? Well, not completely. For the next several years there were drills, assignments, and mini-deployments (hurricane duty). Her tour was ending, and we looked forward to finally resuming our normal lives. Wrong! Near the end of her tour as a National Guardsman, our family was called upon to survive another deployment through stop-loss (the involuntary extension of a service member's active-duty service).

This time we felt like a seasoned military family, prepared for everything—expect the unexpected! This time, we would transfer all calls to my cell phone (no more missed calls!). This time we would purchase more funny greeting cards. This time we would stock up on flat-rate boxes and save funds for postage. This time we would use e-mail for friends and family (repeating everything can be very draining!). This time I would pamper myself and get more sleep. I would learn how to use a digital camera and send Meka more pictures. This time, I wouldn't watch as much news, read as many papers, or use the computer to get more information. (By now, I could write my own Military Mom's Survivor's Guide!) And yes, I would always remember to pray.

My little girl, my "Meka Doll," a veteran and not yet thirty years old, was now Sergeant Harris—her own person, and an excellent soldier. This young woman had made a life decision not only for herself, but for our country. She once explained her life to a younger family member in this way:

"You know the police you see protecting you here in the city as you go about your daily activities? Well, I do just about the same job, only I'm like a police for our country. I protect our country so that everyone is safe."

As I write this, Meka and her unit are still deployed and are not scheduled to return home from theater until the start of 2009. When I talk with her, e-mail, or write, the first thing I say is, "I love you—please remember to pray." And I always include a Bible verse for her to read. I remember how hard it was to release her, to send her off to war. I wanted to hold on to the memories of childhood. But the fear, loneliness, and sleepless nights pale in comparison to the pride I have in Meka's strength and bravery.

Being a military mom has taught me many life lessons. We want our children to grow up to be independent, yet we want our children to depend on us. Being a military mom puts everything in its proper perspective as we accept reality, stay focused in the moment, pray a lot, and believe in our children. We want to keep their spirits up, and we take pride in their positive accomplishments. They are making and living history as we wait for them to come home to tell their part of the story.

So, what do you say when your child decides to join the Army and doesn't ask, "Mother, may I?" You show them your support, and tell them you love them and will always be there for them. And pray—always pray.

Lucky Caswell Harris is a relaxation specialist. She is blessed with two children and two grandchildren. She founded the Mothers of Military (M.O.M.) support network, a program of the USO of Northern Ohio, in 2001, when her daughter joined the Army and Lucky could not locate a support group that met her needs as a mother.

The Most Wonderful Birthday Present

Elizabeth Jameyson

My son deployed to Afghanistan a few years ago, and I didn't have the funds to go see him off. It was heart wrenching for me not to send him off so he would know that he was loved and would be deeply missed. He called from the bus as it was departing the base. He told me, "This is one of the hardest things I've experienced—seeing and listening to all the tearful goodbyes." Even though it would have been incredibly hard to watch him leave, I would have done just about anything to be there and kiss and hug my baby boy before sending him off to war.

I kept my sanity by sending my soldier the best care packages I could send, as often as I could. I joined every Marine Internet site for updates and moral support from other moms who could understand where I was coming from. I made a condolence book for a boy from our town who was killed in Iraq. It was an extremely emotional undertaking for me, but one I wanted to see through and present to the family. A condolence book is begun when a local deployed soldier is killed in action. I immediately went on several of the Marine mom websites I used for information and support. These families responded with beautiful poems, words of comfort, graphics, prayers, and many expressions of honor and sympathy for our fallen soldier.

I uploaded these sentiments and printed them on sheets of decorated scrapbooking paper, arranging them in a binder and adding appropriate stickers to enhance the book's appearance. I ended up with about fifty pages. This book was then presented to the mom during the calling hours for her deceased son. This is truly a heart-wrenching moment, but God gives you the strength to be there and present the book in honor of their soldier's service to our country.

There were other times I sent out condolence letters to individuals who were making the same kind of book for someone in their community who had died serving his country. It helped to stay productive and focus on things I could do and not on things I could not change.

My son stood in tremendously long lines to make a two-minute call home or to be able to use the Internet. Sometimes, he would give up sleep to try when the lines were shorter. I used to leave my instant messaging on all night at the loudest volume to hear when he logged on. It made the sound of a cash register every time he was online because he was always asking me for money!

The best part of his deployment was the homecoming I got the privilege of experiencing when his unit finally came back safe. It was something I will never forget! All the family members were there in their patriotic clothes, carrying banners and balloons and pacing back and forth trying to spot that first bus carrying our soldiers home.

When the buses finally rolled in, I frantically took off to find my son. It seemed forever before I finally found him on one of the last buses to come in. There were so many tears of relief and joy and very long, overdue hugs. I remember a sweet moment when I took a photo of one Marine meeting his baby for the very first time. Months later, I was able to track down that family and send them the photo. It would be my wish that every American could witness a homecoming and experience the joy and gratitude expressed when our troops return safely.

I have quite a different story to tell about my son's second deployment.

"Mom, I've been injured and I'm calling from an Iraqi hospital. Please find Tracy [his wife]. I can't get a hold of her."

These are the words a Marine mom dreads with all her heart and soul.

On October 19, 2005, around noon, my son's unit was on patrol attempting to prevent insurgents from crossing into Iraq from Jordan. The Marines were in an alley, conducting house-to-house searches, when they suddenly heard a car racing toward them. Lance Corporal Anderson, my son's friend, shot the driver. The car detonated, killing Anderson and injuring several other Marines, including my son.

I received the phone call at work, and all I wanted to do was run out of the building, get on the first plane to where my son was, and hold him in my arms.

My soldier told me that every time he heard a loud noise in the hospital, he jumped out of bed and hid underneath it for cover. That broke my heart. His injuries were severe enough to get him transferred to Germany and back to the States.

He came home on a stretcher to his ever-grateful wife and mom. It just happened to be his wife's birthday. His arrival was the most wonderful birthday present! He was able to recuperate at home in Ohio and was very proud to make his very first Thanksgiving turkey dinner for his family. He re-enlisted last summer.

Elizabeth Jameyson raised four daughters and two sons as a single mom, and her life is now filled with the joy of being a grandmother. She works for an accounting firm and also keeps busy maintaining her century home, going to soccer games, and being anywhere she can dance, laugh, and share good times with friends.

When the Cap Is off the Toothpaste

Robin Schaefer

I WILL BE HONEST HERE and admit that I'm not quite sure where to start with this story, only because I'm afraid that once I do, I won't be able to stop. The past five years have brought unbelievable change, both unexpected and unwanted. I have found that I am stronger than I thought I was, that my emotions run deeper than I ever realized, and that I serve a God more loving and merciful than I truly deserve.

My son had never shown *any* interest in the military, so when he came home one afternoon in the summer of 2002, I was completely unprepared for his announcement that he had joined the Army! It was obvious that he had done his research, but I think I would have reacted more positively if I had known ahead of time that he was seriously thinking of doing this. Adam began training in earnest and was set to leave for Fort Leonard Wood in early November. Military police training was at the same base, so he would complete both basic training and AIT (Advanced Infantry Training) before graduation.

On the night before Adam left, we tried to cram four months' worth of family time into one single evening. Our family has always been very close, and before now, we had never even spent more than a weekend apart! Adam's recruiter, realizing how difficult this would be for all of us, gave us a little more time and allowed Adam to remain at home the night before instead of joining the rest of the recruits at a local Holiday Inn. He would come by to pick Adam up at 5:30 A.M., and the rest of us would come by the MEPS (Military Entrance Processing Station) center at 1 P.M. to witness the ceremony and say goodbye. I didn't sleep at all that night. Adam, his brother, and his three sisters had all fallen asleep in the living room after a night of laughter, stories, and board games. I sat on the chair next to the sofa and just watched Adam sleep, cherishing his presence and storing away in my heart every stray hair, every freckle—wondering how I would get through tomorrow, let alone the next four months. Knowing that God does not allow more than He knows we can handle, I gave Adam over to Him and asked for the strength to let go.

The recruiter was a bit late—it was 5:45 A.M. when we finally heard the car pull up in the driveway. Adam walked through the room and gently woke his brother and each of his sisters for a final hug goodbye. He hugged his dad and picked up the small duffel bag that contained the few items he was allowed to take with him. Before he left, he gave me a big hug and whispered, "I love you, Mom. Don't worry, I'll be okay."

Later that afternoon, my husband and I drove down to the MEPS building. We watched—with a roomful of other families—as Adam pledged himself to the military. We stood smiling for pictures, hoping to stretch the time we had left before we had to say a final goodbye. We knew that it would be a while before Adam would be able to contact us again, and that sense of separation was something I had never felt before. We all drove home in deafening silence, and I immediately went downstairs to Adam's room to prove to myself that this was all very real.

Everything was exactly as he left it, clothes strewn about, papers stacked on the desk, remote control waiting by the bed. I sat down at his desk, pulled out a piece of paper, and started to write a letter, even though I had no clue how long it would be before I could actually send it. I had written a mere half of a page before the tears started, and by the time I was ready to go back upstairs, the paper was covered with nothing but ink-colored splotches.

I came up with a number of coping mechanisms during the next few weeks. I ordered a set of dog tags that I wore constantly. One was inscribed with my name and the words "Military Mom." The other simply read "Giving my very best to my country," alongside Psalm 30:5 ("Weeping may endure for a night, but joy comes in the morning"). I also began to wear T-shirts emblazoned with "Military Mom" or "Army Mom." I found that with much prayer, the Lord helped me to handle what I needed to handle.

Adam graduated in March of 2003 and was told that he would be sent immediately to Kuwait. The infamous Army "policy" of "hurry up and wait" kept him around Fort Leonard Wood for three weeks following his graduation. It was such a relief when he found out that plans had changed and he would be going to Schofield Barracks on the island of Oahu, Hawaii, instead of Kuwait!

Talk about a change of venue! Adam was stationed at Schofield for a little over a year when he informed us that his unit was headed for Afghanistan. This was *not* what we wanted to hear, although we had known that technically it was only a matter of time before he deployed. We began counting down the days, and Adam began the specialized training he needed before deployment. However, it was soon apparent that the Lord had something else in mind for my son, because the next time Adam called us it was from the hospital. It seems that there was a mishap during one of the training exercises, and Adam had broken his leg!

After three years in Hawaii, Adam requested a transfer to a base on the mainland, closer to home. It wasn't long before he was told he would be transferred to Fort Drum in New York. He was moving to a garrison unit, so his chances of deployment were low, and this was just fine with me! But just before the move, there was a snafu, and the transfer to Fort Drum was canceled. Now Adam was headed for Fort Riley, Kansas. He was still quite a bit closer to home than when stationed in the middle of the Pacific Ocean, and Adam was able to spend some time with us before reporting to Fort Riley.

It doesn't pay to get complacent, however, about one's chances for deployment. While he was at Fort Riley, Adam was scheduled for deployment several times, but never deployed. It was an emotional roller coaster. I had begun to think that going to war was not in God's plan for Adam. He was less than a year away from completing his enlistment, and he had not decided whether he was going to re-enlist. So, we were very surprised to hear that the 977th Military Police Battalion out of Fort Riley, Kansas, was deploying for Iraq in February of 2007! The whole thing didn't seem real.

Adam came home for Christmas and couldn't wait to show us his new battle dress uniform along with all of the "War on Terror extras." Adam would spend a couple of weeks in Kuwait for more training, and then head to Kirkuk, in northern Iraq, where his battalion would help train Iraqi police. The thing I remember most about that time is that even though I was terrified for my son, I was also so unbelievably proud of him. He was so confident, so ready to go and do what he was trained to do.

When Adam returned to Fort Riley, just a few days after New Year's Day, 2007, I knew that I wouldn't see him again until his unit returned from Iraq. The full realization of what was happening hit me just at that moment. The full realization of what could possibly happen hit me even harder. I was so scared. I knew that I needed to give my son and the whole situation completely over to the Lord—but I had a difficult time handing it over completely.

Adam gave me a hug and said goodbye, and I managed to hold it together—at least until his car was out of sight. I started to cry, and I could not stop—and then I couldn't breathe, and I felt a pain unlike anything I had ever felt before. It was so all-encompassing, so total, I didn't know if I could stand it one more second. But I could, and I did.

All of Adam's things were in storage, and his cell phone was off. The funny thing was that the cell phone affected me most of all. My family has a thing for texting. In fact, I think we tend to text more than talk on our phones. Adam and I used to text several times a day, about odd, random things. It gave us the illusion that he wasn't quite so far away, after all.

Realizing that I would be unable to do this for the next year really hurt. Even though I knew that Adam's phone was no longer functioning, for a few days after he left, I still sent those stupid, random text messages, even though I knew they were going nowhere! While Adam was still home at Christmastime, I used the video feature on my cell phone to create a number of little "Adam moments." I started using these videos as my phone background, so that every time I picked up my phone, I would see my son laughing and saying something silly.

I found a website that sold bracelets for families of soldiers deployed to Iraq that were similar to the old POW bracelets made during the Vietnam War. My bracelet read "Sgt. Adam Schaefer–Army–Operation Iraqi Freedom–2007." In my heart, I made a promise that the bracelet would not come off until Adam came home!

Adam had only been in Kuwait a couple of weeks when he was finally able to call and give us an address—and the news that his deployment had been extended for three additional months!

The post office had recently come out with a priority box in which you could ship items to Iraq for eight dollars, no matter what the weight. We brought a warehouse supply of these, along with the accompanying overseas paperwork, and we would always have one of these boxes open on a table. Whenever we found something we thought Adam might like—whether it was the funnies from the newspaper or a pack of gum—we would throw it in the box, and when it was full, we sent it off. We became experts at stuffing those things! During Adam's first Christmas in Iraq, we sent two boxes with many little numbered packages, along with a paper explaining how to open them. It was a "Christmas from home" package, complete with a little Christmas tree, a favorite ornament, and Christmas cookies.

Not long after Adam arrived in Kirkuk, he informed us that he had purchased a cell phone from a soldier who was returning home. Regular cell phones didn't work there, but these particular phones were similar to prepaid phones and were made for calling home! This phone worked pretty well for a short time, but Adam finally stopped using it because he said it sounded like someone was listening in. The very best way we found to communicate was through online instant messaging. I left my computer on, and whenever Adam would go online, he would check to see if anyone was home. Occasionally, the connection would fail, but it was usually a temporary thing. In order to keep tabs on the time difference, we took a small clock and put it in the living room, set to Iraqi time. This way, we always knew what time it was in Adam's world.

I will admit to two of my phobias while my son was away. The first of these had to do with phone calls. My husband works nights, and so phone calls in the middle of the night are nothing unusual, but whenever a phone call would come in with a name or a number I did not recognize, I would start to tremble. The fear didn't stop until I got some sense that the phone call was in no way related to the Army.

I was also afraid of any unrecognizable car coming up our driveway. Our home happens to be the last house on the street right before a very busy intersection. This means that many, *many* cars use our driveway as a turnaround when they find they are going the wrong way! With each and every unknown car, my heart beat erratically and fell into my stomach.

Fortunately, deployments do end, and Adam's was supposed to end the first week of May 2008. Two weeks before coming home, though, he decided to re-enlist! I will never forget the excitement in his voice when he called to tell us about his unique re-enlistment ceremony held aboard a Black Hawk helicopter!

My son returned home on May 24, 2008. God was faithful and protected him his entire tour, sometimes during very tense and horrendous situations. Right before he came home, I wrote a short poem for him to explain my feelings . . . just as writing my story helps to sort through the roller coaster that is the U.S. military.

When the cap is off the toothpaste
And a duffel's by the door
When a pair of large athletic shoes
Is strewn across the floor
When a bag of used McWrappers
Sits beside the comfy chair
Next to a pair of denim shorts
Too big for me to wear.
When a loud and pounding bass line
Vibrates constant through my feet
When apart from any music
I detect a rhythmic beat
When I sit to watch a movie
Too awake to catch some zzzz's
And I realize I'm missing
All my favorite DVDs
When I sit at my computer
But I cannot get online

And when six distinctive voices
Laugh at some lame joke of mine
My son is home
My son is safe
And everything is fine

Robin Schaefer is an artist and a stay-at-home wife and mom. She and her husband, Ralph, are active advisors in their youth ministry and, along with their five children, are born-again Christians.

Eternity

Penny Norris

IT'S 3 A.M. AND I awake to the sound of our instant messaging service announcing that our son, Kevin, is online. My husband and I bolt out of bed and try not to fall as we hastily descend two flights of stairs to reach the computer. Whenever I hear that sound an incredible sense of relief washes over me. I breathe a little easier, my shoulders relax. "He's safe . . . for this moment he's okay," I think to myself. "Thank you God, he's safe!"

Kevin joined the Marine Corps Reserves in March 2003, as a delayed-entry recruit, the very month we went to war in Iraq. He was a senior in high school. On October 27, 2003, we met three other families at the recruiter's office, and along with them sent our son off to Parris Island for basic training. We supported his decision to join the Corps and were so proud of him that day. Nevertheless, saying goodbye was very difficult for me. I knew it would lead to a more difficult goodbye in the future. I knew that the odds were very likely that his unit would be called to active duty.

He had barely returned from his MOS (military occupational specialty) training in July 2004 when we learned that his unit, the

3rd Battalion, 25th Marines, was being activated and deployed to Iraq in January 2005. This beautiful child my husband and I had brought into the world was now going to be protecting us.

December 2004. The Christmas season was upon us, but I couldn't help wondering if it would be the last one we would celebrate with Kevin. I tried to keep things normal and bake and decorate like every other year. I wanted Kevin to leave home with happy memories of a joyous Christmas, not memories of a tearful mother who tried too hard to make it extra special just in case it was our last together. But normal was the last thing I felt.

Our New Year's didn't feel like cause for celebration, and we spent the week in a fog. Tears were always just under the surface for me, and many times I had to just walk away from a conversation to pull myself together. Shortly before he left, Kevin asked me what I thought eternity would be like. At that moment my heart broke for him. He had been so brave through all these months of preparation, always reminding us that the Corps had trained him well. I didn't realize how much I needed him to be brave, so that I could be brave too. That day our roles were reversed. I tried to remind him of everything our Catholic faith had taught him—that Jesus had died for him and through Him he had a place in heaven. I assured him that we would be together again in eternity, but that he would not miss us because eternity could not be measured by earthly time and that he would never feel alone in the presence of God's love.

January 9, 2005, 4 P.M.: We had spent the last four hours at Kevin's duty station with hundreds of other families, trying to give each other the support we would need for the long months ahead, and now the hour had come to say goodbye. That whole day had been surreal and I spent it not knowing how I was going to leave him there, to send him off to war. Kevin was so strong—I don't know how he held up. One by one he had to hug his brothers, sister-in-law, and dad goodbye. Now it was my turn. Through sobs I told him I loved him and would pray for him constantly. He kissed my left cheek, told me he loved me, and that was it.

This was the moment . . . I forced myself to turn and walk away, every step painful. My legs felt like an odd combination of rubber and lead.

I waited out of earshot for his girlfriend, Colleen. When she reached my side I gathered her in my arms, we turned back for one last look at our handsome Marine, and turned again to take those last dreaded steps to the car and drive home.

January 12, 2005: Kevin called from California, where his unit would be doing some desert training before leaving for Iraq. He was with his "other brothers" and they were focused on their mission and ready to get started. It made me feel so much better to hear him sound so confident and in good spirits.

There is no training for being a Marine mom at war. It's definitely a learn-as-you-go experience. I spent countless hours chatting with other Marine moms (and a few dads) from his battalion on a private website designed for us to be able to support each other. I kept myself busy shopping for goodie box items that I would ship to Kevin every two to three weeks. I didn't watch the news. I refrained from laughing hysterically when other moms tried to compare sending their son or daughter off to college with my experience. Did they really think there was anything remotely the same about it?

Worry was always there lurking in the shadows. Every day when I came home from work I drew a deep breath before I turned the corner onto my street. A sigh of relief . . . no blue government car in the driveway! After a few weeks I realized I had to get my act together. I knew I didn't want to live with worry as a constant companion. I reminded myself that Kevin and all our service men and women are fighting so that we can go about our daily lives without fear. I needed to do my part by living the best life I could live while he was away. Help my neighbor, go to church, work, and have fun. That's the life our sons and daughters are keeping safe for us, and the life they miss and want to return home to. Isn't it interesting that for the period of time they fight to defend our freedom, they lose theirs?

Through Kevin's deployment I developed a closer relationship with God. For the first time in my life I really turned everything over to him. A friend suggested that "all we could do was pray," and in that moment I realized—no, the *best* thing we could do was pray!

Through the prayers and support of so many friends, relatives, and complete strangers, I made it through those long nine months. On October 6, 2005, my Marine came home to all of us who love him. Life will never be the same. I don't take my freedom for granted. I cry every time I have to sing the national anthem. Little things don't upset me like they used to. I know I am the luckiest and most blessed mom in the world!

Penny Norris is a secretary/bookkeeper for an accounting firm. She and her husband, Barry, have three sons. She is an active member of her church, and she enjoys volunteer work, cooking, reading, and Jazzercise.

Shoulder to Shoulder

Debra Estep

I NEVER DREAMED MY AIRMAN, Vince, would deploy to Iraq. When the war broke out, he was in Air Force technical training for his field of computers and networking.

In the spring of 2003, he was sent to his first duty station at Offutt Air Force Base in Nebraska.

In the fall of 2003, he phoned me and asked if I was sitting down. I replied, "Do you think I need to be?" I did not sit down, but he informed me that he had volunteered for a mission to Iraq. He told me he would be guarding third world nationals who entered a U.S. base. My response was "Third world nationals? What are they, prisoners?"

He proceeded to tell me that they were people from other countries who would be working on the U.S. base, but could not be walking around the base without a military escort.

Being in his field of computers and networking, my son had one day of basic training in the weapon he would be carrying, an AK-47 assault rifle. That was a concern of mine. He was not specifically trained for a security detail. He did have an additional eight hours of training with the weapon before he deployed. That did not make me feel much better.

Vincent came home to Ohio for a weekend in early November of 2003. While I was driving him to the airport for his flight back to base, he said to me, "Mom, I have my will and all my papers in order." I did not even glance his way, as my hands were nearly glued to the steering wheel. I said, "Ohhhhh." He proceeded to say, "Mom, we have to do these things." I responded, "I know you do, and I am thankful." My then-nineteen-year-old son proceeded to speak words to me that literally carried me through his deployment. "Mom, even if the very worst was to happen, I want you to know I believe in what I am doing."

Over the months that he was gone, his words, in his voice, echoed in my head. I said them every night as I laid my head down to sleep. It was not until months after his return that I sat down to write.

My son proudly serves
During his deployment
I never once felt alone
First God was at my side
Holding my hand
    Next came family and friends
And my circle enlarged

Around my circle
I envisioned a second
Of other military parents
    And their family and friends
    All standing shoulder to shoulder
Hands clasped with one another

    Around that second circle
I felt the presence
Of the people of the United States of America

With former military folks
Standing just a bit taller than the average person
Each proudly wearing
the dress uniform of their branch

A fourth circle wrapped around
At first I did not fully understand
why they appeared so faint almost transparent
Until I heard their voices

I heard them speak to me
or heard their offered prayers
"Dear God Bless Johnny"
At times I was allowed a glimpse of what their child saw
Battles with men all lined up in rows
Battles of brother fighting brother in the backyards of this country

Troops in foxholes shoulder to shoulder
A harbor on fire
Wounded friends pulled to the safety of floating debris

Soldiers in snow-covered mountains
Soldiers mucking
through humid rice paddies,
Soldiers in blazing heat with sand
whipping their bodies

The voices I heard feminine
The love of a mother
transcends time and space
"We've been where you are now
We've waited months for a single letter home

We've cried your same tears"

You need to know
This was my strength
Knowing I was not alone
Others were standing with me
and others had gone before me

To you whose children have yet to leave
Today is the day you can actually LIVE
Gently call your thoughts back
Remind yourself where they are today

To you whose children are away
Please trust that
We are shoulder to shoulder with you

Debra Estep is currently a stay-at-home mom caring for her youngest son, Kevin. When her son Vince joined the Air Force, he followed in the footsteps of his father, Debra's husband, Michael, who also served in the Air Force. (Vince's wife, Dana Aleandri, also serves in the Air Force.) Debra is involved in online support groups for Air Force parents and for families of our fallen troops.

Living Stories

Saundra Verinece Hunt

ONLY FIVE FOOT THREE, my petite youngest daughter wanted to make a difference. Jasmine wanted to be a police officer. She not only wanted to be an authority and know the law, but also to live it, becoming an example for young people. Although she possessed a strong desire to serve, Jasmine found out in 1998, at age seventeen, that she did not meet the age requirements for the police force. She was too young.

After thinking it over and talking with her dad and me, Jasmine decided instead on the military. She knew her dad would understand. He was a Marine—once a Marine, always a Marine. My youngest daughter chose the Air Force. She was going to take the test just once, and if she didn't pass, she wouldn't take it again. She passed. We had to sign for her to be able to enlist.

I remember sitting on the floor in her room, crying, and my husband sitting down beside me. I remember the feeling like it was yesterday. I knew that if we ever went to war, my sweet baby girl, the one who played with Cabbage Patch dolls and My Pretty Pony, would probably have to go. Oh, I needed support—and there were no support groups around. How horrible!

I had a whole year to think about my daughter going into the Air Force, because she was in the delayed-entry program. On September 10, 1998, Jasmine turned eighteen years old. On September 15, she was on her way to basic training in Texas, all one hundred pounds of her. She wanted to be a security police officer, but she ended up changing her MOS (military occupational specialty) to administration. After she successfully completed boot camp, Jasmine's first duty station was at Holloman Air Force Base in New Mexico. She had been serving there for three years when another child of mine decided to make a difference.

James said, "Mom and Dad, I am going to talk to the Marines, but I'm not joining."

When he came back home, he was smiling and he said, "I joined and I'm going to be a mortarman."

His dad, James Sr., said, "No." I said, "Is that what I think it is?"

A mortarman and his team are on the front line of dealing with the threat of indirect fire when insurgents attack. When attacked with mortars, the Marine mortarman and his team respond with mortars of their own. We had questions—lots of questions.

I called the Marine recruiter's office. Gunny (Gunnery Sergeant) Corvin answered. "My son joined the Marines and is going to be a mortarman," I told him. "Is that what I think it is?"

"Yes," Gunny Corvin answered.

James didn't even know what a mortarman was. He just remembered hearing "weekend duty" and "reserves." After some discussion, James changed his MOS to active-duty administration. When James went to Parris Island in 2001, I had two hearts in the military—my two children, both serving. James made it through boot camp, becoming a fourth-generation Marine. After more schooling and training, his first duty station was Okinawa, Japan, for one year.

After 9/11, Jasmine wasn't the only one scared to have her brother in the Marines. Once again I felt that need to connect with other families. I needed support. This time I felt I knew something. I had learned from my experience of having Jasmine in the service. This knowledge could help not only my children, but other families as well.

I felt a tug at my heart. A support group was needed. I shared my ideas with Dr. Alicia Malone, an Air Force mom, and Mona Bennett, my children's godmother. Alicia asked me, "Saundra, what are you going to do? Are you going to start a support group or let it fall by the wayside?"

I answered, "I'm going to do it!"

And, thanks to Mona and Alicia, I did.

What would we be called? Since it takes all branches, strong and brave, to make up our military, we are called the Family and Friends Connected Military Support Group, a nonprofit organization. Our connection is that we all have or know someone who is serving in the military. Mona has stood by my side since the beginning of the group, becoming my administrative assistant.

We bring together active-duty armed forces members, their families, and their friends to bear up and sustain one another. We serve families from Akron, Barberton, Canton, Cleveland, Cuyahoga Falls, Copley, Dover, Hartville, Hudson, Stow, Tallmadge, and Wadsworth, Ohio.

We are living stories. Having a place to come, knowing it's all right to feel the way you do, and knowing that we stand together—this is what our support group is all about. We live this military family life each and every day. On November 9, 2008, we will be seven years old. We've met every month—sometimes twice a month.

Each month, we have a ceremony called Lights of Hope. During the ceremony, we use candles, but we don't light them—with either a match or lighter—because we don't want the lights ever to go out. And we don't use candles with electric lights, because even those would go out when the switch was turned off.

LIGHTS OF HOPE

We stand in the gap for our military families
The wicks on our candles are not lit
By a match or a lighter
Our lights of hope
Are lit by the flames of our heart
For as long as our hearts beat
Our lights of hope will shine bright
We stand in the gap for those we lost
On September 11
In New York, Pennsylvania, and the Pentagon
We stand in the gap for those we lost
In Enduring Freedom and Operation Iraqi Freedom
And yes, we stand in the gap
For those who are standing watch over us
So proud and brave
Stateside and abroad
Like a beacon of light
Guiding the ships home
For as long as our hearts beat
Our Lights of Hope will shine bright
For we are the true Lights of Hope.
We stand Strong.

I am so thankful for each and every family that has allowed me to stand with them. I thank my two hearts, James and Jasmine, for their service to our country. God bless them.

Saundra Verinece Hunt was told at a young age that she would never have children. Nonetheless, she and her husband, James, have two children, and now delight in being grandparents. Saundra is the founder and director of Family and Friends Connected Military Support Group (www.familyfriendsconnected.com), which provides links to a variety of free support services for military families.

Only Child

Karen Phelps

SHE WAS SEVENTEEN, AND I was a basket case. She graduated from high school in 1994 and by the end of the month was at the Air Force Academy. Basic training lasted six weeks. Thank goodness, we had always primitive camped—the dirt, bugs, heat, and tents did not bother her. She spent her eighteenth birthday learning to shoot an M-16!

Since graduating from the Air Force Academy in 1998, she has lived and served in the Air Force all over the world. Now an Air Force major, my daughter has been on active duty for more than ten years. She works in the civil engineering squadron, playing in the dirt and with big trucks, building things. That is what I tell people about her—my one and only, beloved daughter.

After a three-month deployment to Egypt in 1999–2000 for a multinational exercise, a one-year remote to South Korea, and tours of duty to Italy and Germany, I thought I was prepared for her deployment to Kuwait in August of 2006. I was thinking of her deployment as just another assignment around the world, with a chance to live in a new place and meet new people. Having spent time in the desert in Egypt, she knew about the sandstorms, lack of water, and camping out.

My daughter was stationed in Germany and came back to the States for CST (combat survival training) at Fort Sill, Oklahoma. She and fifty other Air Force personnel were going to Kuwait to help run an Army base. She said she would be the base CE (civil engineer), helping to keep the electricity and water running. We got to see her for three days before she was deployed. One of my favorite sayings is "Knowledge is power." So I always try to find out as much as I can about a new base or country. It makes my daughter feel that much closer to us.

Every day since my daughter has been in the Air Force, I say a prayer for her, taking one day at a time. When she was deployed to Kuwait I knew she was well trained and would be safe. We received weekly phone calls. She sounded tired, but okay. We looked for her special short e-mails saying, "Hi, Doing well. Talk soon. Love you. Me."

We send goodie boxes and tons of cards, and the only things she's asked for—salt-and-vinegar chips and plain, dark-colored flip-flops. Try to find plain, dark-colored flip-flops in October in Ohio—you can't. I finally e-mailed an Army mom friend in Florida, who sent out a box. We even mailed out a Green Bean Coffee Card so that she could enjoy a good cup of coffee each day.

On Christmas Day, we were lucky to get a phone call. Like so many Christmas Days through the years, even though we were separated, we opened our gifts together over the phone. The call was going well until she said she might be changing bases because she was needed somewhere else. Of course no information was given, which sent me into my "fret and worry" mode. My daughter always knows it is better to let me know things after the fact. For example, when she was still at the Academy, she sent me a video that I thought was from her church mission work in Arizona. Nope, it was her falling out of a perfectly good airplane—

five times—to earn her jump wings. My heart almost stopped on that one.

We got another quick phone call telling us she was now stationed in Iraq. Iraq! I was not prepared for Iraq. It was like getting hit in the stomach and not knowing where to turn. She was based in Baghdad, but was traveling all over the country with a group of multinational environmental people. *What?* Flying all over Iraq in a helicopter? My only child?! I felt like there was a cloud hanging over my head. I had always been strong about Jen being gone. But this time, things were different. Sending your only child, and daughter, off to war is not like sending your child to college.

My daughter returned to Germany in April 2007, safe and sound and ten pounds lighter. When she came back home to Ohio for a visit, we finally learned a little bit about her time in Iraq—of course they can never tell you everything. She and her unit would fly to remote bases all over Iraq to start the environmental cleanup process. She ran into some "Red Horse" (Rapid Engineer Deployable Heavy Operational Repair Squadron Engineers) personnel from her South Korean tour and got to see the oasis at the Al Asad base that's mentioned in the Bible.

My daughter gave us some beautiful pictures taken in Kuwait and Iraq. I keep a record of all her travels. Being stationed overseas, my daughter has taken advantage of the opportunity to see the world. She has picked up a smattering of languages and a love of strong coffee. She is still stationed in Germany until her next assignment, starting the summer of 2009.

My daughter and I both share a love of God, history, travel, and books. I've been able to travel to Italy and Germany to visit Jen. We toured the Normandy beaches, the cemeteries at Omaha Beach, and the American cemetery in Luxembourg to honor the fallen from the Battle of the Bulge. I know my daughter, Major Jen Phelps, is proud to serve in the United States Air Force, and we are so proud of her.

I'm blessed with the greatest family and friends. They got me through really tough times. I received a lot of hugs, prayers, and phone calls so I would not become a "nut case." I joined up with a wonderful support group in Akron, called Family and Friends Connected Military Support Group. I needed to be around people who had a clue as to how I was feeling—people who had their own children in the services and deployed in Iraq. We meet once a month and get phone calls from the founder, Saundra Hunt. At the meetings, we have guests who talk about subjects regarding the military, deployments, and families left at home. We are the parents, wives, husbands, and siblings of our military family. I have been attending the meetings for a year and a half. They have really helped me cope. Our thoughts and prayers go out to everyone still serving in Iraq and Afghanistan.

Karen Phelps has been married to her husband, Gale, for thirty-eight years. She enjoys reading, gardening, and camping. She also loves travel; when she visited her daughter in Europe, they had the honor of visiting the cemeteries at Omaha Beach and the American Cemetery in Luxembourg honoring those fallen in the Battle of the Bulge. Karen donates blood every fifty-seven days because her mother received many transfusions that prolonged her life.

A Christmas Miracle

Wendy Anderson

"PLEASE DON'T DO THIS, Derek. You are seventeen years old. I'm not ready to let you go. You're still in school. Not yet."

"I have to, Mom. I gave my word," he said. Then he looked at the recruiter sitting in my living room, a Marine who had befriended him at school. I studied Derek's face. He had given his word. He is honorable. He would sign on in two months, when he turned eighteen, with or without my permission. I signed the papers. He picked up his duffel bag, and they were gone.

He finished his last year of high school here and graduated in June 2005. All the while, the Marines and the war were waiting in the wings, and heavy on my mind. He left for boot camp September 6, 2005.

He excelled in his job, as I knew he would. He had earned his "expert" rifleman status before he graduated boot camp. Sitting in the bleachers, watching him graduate, I felt a pride in him that cannot be put into words—and a pride in myself. *I did that.* I set an example, and I gave him tools as a child to be the man he wanted to be.

Infantry training flew by and he was assigned a permanent

base. Kaneohe Bay, Hawaii. Far. He wasn't there long. He was deployed to Iraq in September 2006. He was going to Haditha in Anbar province, where things were still unsettled. Where the Marines were still fighting. Full-blown combat, every . . . single . . . day.

I was with him in Hawaii when he left. The cost of a flight didn't matter. Nothing mattered, except that I be there. We didn't talk much. We didn't have to. He knew that I was going with him, in spirit. And I would never leave his side. I would walk with him.

The courage he had to walk away with his platoon, to walk into that danger, is courage that I will never know. What I did know is that I would never see him again. I don't mean literally. I mean I would never see *that* Derek again. He would be different.

The soldiers in Haditha at that time didn't have the setup they do now. They had the hardships of getting the area settled. They fought every day. He didn't have a cot; he lay on the ground when he could, which wasn't often. He had no running water or electricity. He just patrolled and fought. He washed and brushed his teeth four or five times during his seven-month tour. They ate when the supply truck could get to them.

Once a month, a truck would bring a satellite phone out, so the soldiers could call home. Usually, the connection wasn't good enough to talk, but I could hear his voice. I knew that that day, he was okay. They weren't dressed warm enough and froze during that winter. Twenty-three Marines in his battalion were killed. I don't know how many were wounded.

Because they were out in the field and not on a base, they had no PX (post exchange) to buy supplies. This cost my husband and me financially. We sent boxes of nutritious food—enough for the soldiers who weren't getting boxes. We sent gloves and hoods for them to stay warm, and what seemed like hundreds of socks and pairs of underwear. They couldn't wash their clothes or socks. They peeled them off after two weeks and threw them away, so we would send more. They got trench foot. I sent boxes of foot medicine. The whole platoon had bowel upsets. I sent tons of medicine for that. We sent them everything we could think of to help, regardless of the cost.

For me here, everyday life totally changed. Through my years as a mother, I was the protector. That control and ability to protect my son was taken away from me, and in the hands of men I didn't know. Men I had to blindly trust to watch his back. I was helpless to protect him. So I was afraid—every day, every night, every minute.

I kept my cell phone on, and on me at all times. I never turned it off—at a meeting, or a church, a doctor's office, or at night. Never. I told Derek if he ever called, I would be on the other end. And I was. Always.

I also carried with me what I can only describe as an invisible time bomb. No one could see it. I couldn't see it. I could feel it. It was heavy. It was fear. Tick. Tick. It wasn't necessarily going to go off, but it could. I didn't know. My life could change in a split second. Would it? No. Push it away. I can't. Tick. Tick. So I sent a white light to him, my soldier, through my mind and my heart. I visualized a white light, surrounding him, protecting him. It was all I *could* do. Every day.

I have a very special mouse, given to me by my mother as a Christmas present when I left home and moved into my first apartment. He is also special to Derek. The mouse, made of glass, is smaller than a pea, and although he is over thirty years old, he is not chipped or cracked. The mouse is still perfect. And he only comes out at Christmas.

As a child, Derek would look for that mouse when we unwrapped our ornaments every year. While his brothers grabbed the biggest, brightest decorations, Derek would take the little mouse gently out of his cotton ball and marvel at him. "How can this be, Mom? We lose our jackets, our shoes and our car keys, but we have never lost this mouse. And he is so small!" "I don't know," I would say. "It's a Christmas miracle."

When Christmas came and Derek was in Iraq, that is what I sent him. I know a man his age doesn't need a glass mouse. But he did need a piece of home. My husband was afraid for me. He told me I would never see that mouse again. I put the mouse in his cotton ball and sent him overseas.

A few days after Christmas, Derek called. "I knew it!" he said. "I knew when I saw cotton, that mouse was in there! But Mom, I don't have anyplace . . ."

"It doesn't matter, son. The mouse doesn't matter to me. The only thing that matters is that you have *home*. If you can only hang on to him for one day, that's enough."

And so the days dragged on. I cried a lot. I had difficulty sleeping. Sometimes I would jerk awake, thinking I had heard him. I went into his room sometimes to smell his clothes. I had trouble grocery shopping, because I couldn't go down certain aisles and see his favorite things without crying. I thought I was going crazy. It took a toll on my marriage. Why doesn't my husband help me? Make me feel better? I didn't realize he couldn't. He couldn't feel what I felt. He is not a mother.

At what I felt was my breaking point, I was rescued. Saundra Hunt called me to join her group, Family and Friends Connected. It was there I found that I was not crazy. There were mothers who smelled their kid's clothes, who couldn't sleep, who couldn't go down the cereal aisle anymore, and who cried a lot. And it was okay to feel that way.

Derek came back to his base in Hawaii in April 2007. I was there, standing next to the runway when his plane landed. I waited as the steps were pushed to the plane. Then he was walking down them, with his rifle and a backpack on. He was whole and well. Once I put my arms around him, I didn't want to let him go. It was heaven. He stood for that about half a minute! He placed his backpack on the ground, dug around in it a second, then stood back up and handed me my mouse. It had been to war and back, and it was perfect. It was a miracle.

Wendy Anderson is a wife and mother of three sons. For thirty years she has been a nurse, paramedic, firefighter, and volunteer. Her most difficult but proudest assignment was working at Ground Zero after 9/11, rendering first aid to the firemen and construction workers for three weeks.

Tracks in the Sand

Renie Martin

I GAVE JIMMY A BIG, long hug at the front door as we said good-bye. Wondering how long I could hold on, I heard him say, "Mom, don't worry. The Marines are trained to do what we're going to do. It will be okay." I knew he was searching for words to comfort a mother's worry. Boy, what a turnaround. I was supposed to tell him everything would be all right, as I did many times when he was growing up, as he walked out our front door into that big world. I had to squeeze him ever so tight to convince him and myself that I'd be strong for him and that everything would be okay.

It was called Operation Iraqi Freedom. Jimmy was going to the Middle East with a fleet of five ships from Virginia with the Marines from Camp Lejeune, North Carolina. They traveled with their amphibious assault vehicles (AAVs)—their "tracks," as they called them.

We bought our first computer so we could communicate by e-mail. Jimmy later wrote that the lines to the computers were very long and took hours of waiting. It was okay. Go relax, son, or go do what Marines do on ships. You'll have some big days ahead of you. Don't worry about us. It's our job to worry about you. So we waited impatiently for letters from Jimmy to let us know what he was doing and what was going on. Our first letter came.

> January 15, 2003
> Dear Family,
> What's up? Well, I'm on the ship. Tomorrow we face east and pump out for the desert. It'll take us 30 days to get there. We're going through the Suez Canal. It's an unscheduled visit. They don't know we're coming through, and we're pretty sure they won't be too happy with 5 American warships just cruising through, full of Marines.
> Well, need to squeeze in the shower and hit the rack.
> Love always and forever,
> James B. Martin LCpl/USMC

The question of every day became "Did a letter come?" There is nothing like reading letters from your Marine, seeing all of this from his point of view. He wrote about the well deck, where all the vehicles and equipment were stored, and how awesome it was to look at all the power they had in just one ship. They were ready! Ooorah! Boy was that good to hear! Ending one of his letters he wrote, "I'm out doing the thing right now. I love my country and what we stand for, and I owe this to her for all she's done for me. I'm proud to do it and you'll never hear me bitch about going. Don't worry. Love you to death . . . That flag better be flying!"

The computer gave us another connection to Jimmy. A fellow Marine mom shared the Internet site of a reporter from a Virginia newspaper who was on a ship with Marines heading for the Middle East. He was writing of their experiences on the ship. As the reporter wrote about an article a week, we waited for Jimmy's letters. His letters and the articles were quite similar. Then it hit me hard. "Oh my gosh, he's with the same fleet as Jimmy!" He was the missing link that I was looking for to make a real connection to

Jimmy and to what was happening. After all, I never had to send a son to war before, and I needed something real. A reporter—this was real!

I was new at searching the Internet, but I learned quickly. I became obsessed with searching every topic related to Jimmy's deployment: the Marine Corps, amphibious assault vehicles, Camp Lejeune, Navy ships, and maps of Iraq and Kuwait. I wanted to learn everything I could about what my son was experiencing. I wanted to try to be there with him, I guess, and in some weird way I felt that I was doing something. I also think that keeping my mind busy kept my heart away from the fears of the unknown.

I heard other Marine moms tell me what camps their sons were at in Kuwait. Once Jimmy's fleet landed, I tried to figure out what camp he was in. I never could figure that out, but I was able to find platoon pictures on the Camp Lejeune website. I looked and looked at each of the faces and zoomed in to try and find my Jimmy. Those boys looked hot and tired under their "boony" hats. I narrowed it down to two pictures. I picked the one that came closest and pinned it on my wall at work. I felt like my boy was with me.

On Wednesday, March 19, 2003, at 9:54 P.M. EST (but who's keeping track?), "the operation" began. While we were home, the TV was on constantly. Each news station had its own trademark title and soundtrack. It was jarring, hypnotizing, and frightening, each network competing for our hunger for information about what was happening. Jimmy's younger brother, Zak, then thirteen, said the opening music sounded like death. In a weird way, he was right. I could understand and respect his honesty. It was quite sobering to think of all this through the eyes of a younger sibling. Neighbors invited Zak to go to Florida with them. It was an escape that he needed.

I was afraid of so many things once they got rolling, other than the obvious. How would the desert heat affect the troops? I hope they stayed hydrated. What would the encounters with the Iraqi people be like? We didn't know them. We didn't know about the chemicals that Saddam might have. If they were exposed to them, what would the short- and long-term effects be? What about Saddam's Republican Guard? How many? How bad? This thought was going through my mind over and over: these were our boys who just yesterday were playing war video games. It wasn't fun and games anymore. It was war. It was real this time—no stopping the game, no turning it off, no extra lives.

The first days of the operation were under way, the "on your mark, get set, go," as I call it. I still didn't know where Jimmy was exactly or what group he was with. Was it the 1st or 2nd division? Which battalion? Company A, B, or C? The Marines were heading north to Baghdad. They were moving so swiftly that their supply line couldn't keep up with them. Time to worry again. Their food and water could be days behind them. And there were sandstorms. And they weren't getting enough sleep. And they had to fight an enemy out there somewhere.

On Sunday morning I woke up, turned on the television, and went to my usual place at the computer, hoping to find a new article from my pal, the embedded (remember that word?) reporter. I started watching a cable news station and saw words scrolling across the bottom of the screen. The 507th Maintenance Company had gone off course and was ambushed. Lives were lost, hostages were taken, and some were missing.

A Marine unit named Task Force Tarawa had also gone into An Nasiriyah and was attacked, with ten believed killed. My first thought was "No, it couldn't be." Then I started thinking about the articles I had read and the timetable for Jimmy's arrival in Iraq. From everything I'd been looking at, it could have taken them four days to get there. It could take that amount of time . . . it was possible . . . it was more than possible. Suddenly I thought, "Oh my God! It's Jimmy. I know he's there!"

"JIM!" I yelled to my husband as I ran down the stairs. "He's there. I know he's there. I know it's his group. It's called Task Force Tarawa. That's what the reporter is talking about in his articles. I know he's there. Oh my God! Oh my God!" We stared at the television. The scrolling continued. Then the feeling of true fright hit us both. I didn't know what to say next. I felt frozen. I don't know what I'd do if anything happened to Jimmy, I thought as we stared at the TV. "I was always able to help my son, but now I can't." These words came from Jim with much difficulty. Jim and I held each other. Then he said something that was so surreal. "We just have to wait for either a phone call or a white car to come to the house. If they don't, then he's okay." We got neither.

First letter after An Nasiriyah, postmarked March 31:

Dear Family,

By now you've watched CNN and heard about the fighting in An Nasiriyah. I'm OK. Yes, I was in the middle of it all. CNN called it the worst fighting since Nam. They're right. It was ugly. I will make it home so don't start freaking!.

Just pray for the families of my brothers who didn't make it out of that hell hole. They're gone but can NEVER be forgotten. I know I'll never forget them. They sacrificed all for everyone back home.

Bottom line, I'm alive, healthy and unscathed. Thought you'd like to know. Gotta keep fightin', duckin', runnin', and gunnin'! Love you all and miss you! God Bless America.

Your son,

Jimmy

We didn't get any letters for a long time after that one. Of course we didn't. They were in the middle of what I called a war, not an operation. That was too nice a word. I continued to hold close to me what Jimmy had said before he left, that the Marines are the best, and that they are the best trained. Yes, they are!

I had heard that there was a Camp Lejeune liaison. I called him during my lunch hour to ask how Lance Corporal James Martin was doing. I know this was stupid and I usually tried not to be a meddling mother, but I couldn't help it, and I didn't care. The Marine on the other end said, "Ma'am, he's fine. What you need to do is go and have a good lunch, get a good night's rest, and stop watching the news." He was right. It's the best advice I had gotten.

One day a neighbor asked me how Jimmy was doing. Then she said, "I don't know how you do it. I couldn't do it." To this day I think about that statement. How did I do it? You just do. In the evening when I took a walk I would look at Mr. Moon and know that it was the same moon Jimmy was looking at halfway around the world. And there is nothing that makes you feel stronger than being surrounded by American flags everywhere, painted on cars, hanging on fences, in yards, on lapels. I left the Christmas candles in the window from when Jimmy was home, before he was deployed. I turned them on every night so the light would guide him back home. Neighbors helped me put up yellow ribbons on the freeway overpass to remind us of our troops. Humor helped too. Women at work were talking and wanted to help the cause. Let the moms fight! We would dress in burkas and underneath would be our M16 rifles and chocolate. We would rotate out every twenty-eight days, when we had PMS. We figured they would surrender real quick!

How did I do it? I think about that question. I think we all did it. I think it was Jimmy's friends who came over evenings and sat with us. It was strangers who asked about Jimmy and said they would keep him in their thoughts and prayers. It was bosses and coworkers who listened. It was other Marine moms. It was Aunt Lea, who called and asked how Jim-Jam was. It was the friend who put a yellow ribbon on every tree in the neighborhood so Jimmy could see them when he drove up our street when he came home. It was the red, white, and blue afghan knitted by a friend "to comfort me while Jimmy was away." It was family on call 24/7. It was the first-grader who wrote to Jimmy, "I hope you are safe. PS. Call me, 440-123-4567. Love, Tommy." When Corporal James B. Martin got home, he did call Tommy. But the real question isn't "How did I do it?" The real question is "How did they do it?"

They were Task Force Tarawa. They fought one of the fiercest battles in Iraq and secured the bridges of An Nasiriyah. They assisted in the rescue of Jessica Lynch and played a part in the retrieval of the hostages of the 507th Maintenance Company. The 2nd Marine Expeditionary Brigade, 2nd Marine Division, 1st Battalion received the Presidential Unit Citation, which hadn't been awarded since the Vietnam War. They certainly did what they went to do. The tracks to An Nasiriyah have long been blown away in the desert sand, but the tracks from this experience will stay in our hearts and minds forever.

"Some gave all, all gave some."
We'll NEVER forget, rest in peace, brothers,
We miss you. Semper Fidelis.

Renie Martin is not a writer; just a mom who is proud and honored to tell her story so that others might understand what it is like to send a child to war. She hopes that someday there can be peace so that moms around the world won't have to tell this same story over and over and over again.

The Cross, the Little Bible, and the St. Christopher Medal

Laura Gavlak

WHEN I FIRST FOUND out my son, Bret, was going to Iraq from August 2005 to February 2006, I did not want to tell my parents. They are getting older and I did not want them to worry. Being a Marine mom, I did find the courage to tell them. I tried to be strong but I could not hold back the tears. I wondered how I was going to get through the deployment. I knew that my Catholic faith and prayer would be the only way for me to cope. I prayed in the car, in the shower, in the garden, and in my sleep. Iraq would creep into my head constantly. Wake up—Iraq. All day—Iraq. Sleep—Iraq.

During his first deployment, my son was a mechanic on the Light Armored Vehicles (LAVs) and Humvees. He was busy, but found time to call or e-mail home. On December 8, 2005, while I was e-mailing my son, he e-mailed me right back. We went back and forth as if he were in the next room. I ended our session by telling him to get to bed (it was 2 A.M. Iraqi time). "You are half-way around the world and your mom can still tell you what to do!"

He wrote back and got one up on me by writing, "Aren't you at work? You should get to work. I am on the other side of the world and know what you are doing!" It was a great day! This did not happen again because of the eight-hour time difference.

Another wonderful moment was Tuesday, December 19, 2005. My son sent pictures from Iraq via e-mail. I remember looking at the pictures and feeling as though Bret were right there in the room with me—looking good in his cammies, smiling. I sure did miss him and I am so grateful for computer technology.

My everyday routine had changed. During a deployment, my first thought of the day was "Please God, keep Bret safe." I also found the wonderful website Marineparents.com, where I could talk with other parents. I learned so much from reading their stories, and I knew I had a wealth of support close by. I also mailed a care package once a week, every week, for seven months for both deployments.

When I had a sick feeling in my stomach and couldn't sleep, I would cross-stitch. I stitched and prayed and finished a project in seven months. I gave the picture to my son. Besides cross-stitching, I feel that it is important what you do with your time while your loved one is deployed. I stayed busy and got into the Operation PAL (Prayers and Letters for Injured Marines) program, making cards and writing letters (website: http://www.operationpal.com).

The holidays are not the same when a family member is not home. At Thanksgiving I set a place at the table for my son, even though he was in Iraq. Every year there is a table setting in honor of our troops who cannot be home with their families, signifying the sacrifices of our military on our behalf.

For Christmas I decided I would bake cookies and send them to Iraq. The Nestlé website has "desert-safe" recipes using ingredients that will not spoil, even though it takes seven to fourteen days for a package to arrive in Iraq.

The cookies were a hit with the guys. Bret called and said, "Send more cookies because I only got one [cookie)]." I baked cookies for a month and had fun doing it. I was determined that every Marine was going to have Christmas cookies. I knew this feat was impossible, but I mailed as many boxes as I could.

I counted down the days until my son's battalion made it home safely. The excitement was building, and the spring in my step was back. It was exciting to pick him up at the airport. The sick feeling in my stomach had vanished too.

Then came the news of deployment number two: Bret would be going back to Iraq from February 2007 to September 2007. I remember I was washing dishes and Bret told me, "I am going to Fallujah soon. I will be providing security with the MPs."

I said, "That sounds a little dangerous." He replied, "It is a lot dangerous." I knew what that meant: convoys and the ever-constant worry of roadside bombs. I knew his job meant serious business, and that this was going to be a tough deployment. The sick feeling came back.

Before Bret left, I gave him my St. Christopher (patron saint of travelers) medal, which my mom gave to me when I was a little girl. I told him, "Put the medal in your flak jacket." I placed the Little Bible (given to Bret by his cousin Greg, from Greg's mom) in his seabag. The Little Bible went to Vietnam once and to Iraq twice. I made twelve crosses out of dried palms from church. I laminated the crosses and told Bret to put them in the Humvees. Bret carried a cross in his pocket every day.

After Bret made it to Camp Fallujah, we would get a phone call when he wasn't busy. There was no Internet this time. Sometimes Bret would only call once a month, and I would write it on the calendar. He worked long hours in the extreme heat. During one of the calls home, he said, "It has been over one hundred degrees for a hundred days straight."

Once again keeping myself busy, I was on the lookout for things to send in the weekly care package. I sent fans, neck coolers, boot insoles, socks, socks, and more socks. I sent foot spray, wet wipes, goodies, and handheld games.

At the halfway point of deployment number two, I started making plans to go to the homecoming at Camp Lejeune. September 22, 2007, was one of the best days of my life—my son again came home safely from Iraq. I struggled with many emotions that day. I was happy, but I kept thinking about the parents who lost a son. I have the utmost respect for the Gold Star parents. They have a heavy cross to bear and it is heartbreaking, as their sons paid a dear price for our freedom. We must never forget these heroes.

A military homecoming is a sight to see. The excitement and anticipation are enough to make a person explode. To see the buses rolling in full of happy Marines is awesome. Seeing everyone hugging and kissing and smiling is what it is all about.

Bret gave back the cross. It was so tattered. I still get choked up about the cross, the Little Bible, and the St. Christopher medal. They all came back with him. I am forever changed by the deployments to Iraq, and so is my son. I am kinder to people, as everyone is fighting some kind of battle. Understanding and patience go a long way. I appreciate what an awesome military we have protecting us. Thank you, troops!

Sergeant Bret Gavlak will be in active duty until May 2012.

Laura Gavlak works full-time as an office manager. She and her husband, Don, have two sons and one grandchild. Her favorite hobbies are rubber-stamping, cross-stitching, and reading, and Laura continues to send care packages to Marines in the Middle East.

Online Banking

Karen White

LIKE MANY MOMS, I have to show a brave front to my coworkers and friends, my family members, and especially to my son. So it's not often that I'm given the opportunity to unload my feelings like this.

February 14, 2007, is the date that my son, Dan (age eighteen), went off with his Army recruiter to begin his journey into the U.S. Army. The first few months flew by quickly, and before we knew it, my husband and I were at Fort Sill, Oklahoma, for Dan's graduation from boot camp. What a proud day that was. We were so happy to see him in his uniform standing tall and confident. We bought the boot camp video and the souvenir coffee mug and toured the camp.

During the graduation weekend, Dan's boot camp buddies who had joined the National Guard told him, one by one, "I'm going to Iraq in November" "I'm headed over to Iraq in October." I thought to myself, "Thank God, Dan's not in the National Guard; there's no way he'll be going anywhere for quite some time."

Quite some time came way too quickly. Dan went off to his permanent assignment at Fort Polk, Louisiana, shortly after his advanced classes at Fort Sill. He arrived at Fort Polk in August. By mid-August, he called and told us he was coming home on mandatory leave in October because he was going to Kuwait in November and then on to Iraq. What? This couldn't be. It was too soon. He was too young.

October 2007 came really fast, and Dan was home and gone before we could blink. The day following Thanksgiving, Dan's platoon left for Kuwait. Okay, I thought. He'll be in Kuwait, a relatively safe place, until probably January or February 2008.

Nope. The week before Christmas I got a call. "Mom, we're leaving for Iraq. I can't tell you when, but real soon. I love you." I cried. It was the worst Christmas ever. We didn't hear from him again until sometime in January.

When he got to Iraq, I didn't know where he was. Of course, I told myself he was in the "safe" Green Zone and he'd be just fine. Nope again. We would come to find out he was in Baghdad—Camp Rustamiyah. As soon as I found out where he was I began my Internet search and found out everything I could about his location.

Thank God for the Internet. Thank God for e-mail, but damn for the newspaper. Something makes me read it every day. They report every day about the deaths that occurred the day before. I scan the deaths first for words like Fort Polk, Rustamiyah, and "southeast of Baghdad." Every day there is a knot in my stomach.

Throughout his time in Iraq so far, Dan had told me in every phone call that he hadn't left base. He was fine, and even bored. He would tell me, "We're doing nothing at all." Then I looked on the Internet again when my daughter came home for Easter and showed me his MySpace page. There were lots of pictures of Dan, not on base but outside of the base—outside the wire. Wait a minute. I guess he's just trying to protect me.

During the weeks that I don't hear from him, I look at his online banking to see if he's made transactions. The small purchases that he makes assure me that he's okay. I feel guilty for living my day-to-day life. He's constantly on my mind in everything I do.

My daughter doesn't understand. "Danny, Danny, Danny. That's all you ever talk about. What about me, Mom?" She's a twenty-one-year-old senior at Ohio Northern. She's doing very well, and she's safe because of Dan and his buddies.

My husband and I have a weekend cottage on a lake and a boat. We go out on the boat and I think to myself, "I can only do this because Dan and his friends are protecting me." I feel proud and honored. Then I think, "Here I am swimming in the cool water. It's 117 degrees in Iraq, dusty, sandy, and scary." The guilt again—it's a yo-yo.

I've never told anyone this, but I do fear the arrival of a U.S. Army car in our driveway. Sometimes when my husband and I are away for a weekend, I think, "What if the Army is trying to contact us?" "What if something has happened to Dan?" "We should be home." Those are thoughts that I have to push way, way, way back into my mind and deep into my throat so that they never come up. Only positive thoughts are permitted to be sent into the universe.

I also worry that Dan will never see our twelve-year-old golden retriever again. That would be so sad. It's July 1 now. He turns twenty at the end of August. He's not due to return permanently to Fort Polk until next January. He is coming home in September for a mid-tour leave. I can't wait, and neither can he.

I can visualize him coming down the runway at Cleveland Hopkins International Airport and giving me a big "soldier-like" hug. I'll cry. Sob, really. My husband and daughter will cry too. We'll all be so happy to see him and to be able to hold on to him for a couple of weeks. I know he'll come home and sleep in his room, in his bed for at least twenty-four hours straight. He'll be twenty, but I'll still peek in the room to watch him sleep.

Just a boy, I'll think—such a man, really. I'll show him the album of all the e-mails that I've printed off and saved.

My daughter says that it's so "stalkerish" that I print and save his e-mails. I consider that it's more like the equivalent to when the mothers of World War II soldiers received letters from their sons. They kept those. I keep the e-mails. "Same thing," I tell her. I also print and keep the pictures from his MySpace page. It's all I have, and I'm not embarrassed.

I sign off on every e-mail with "I love you. Stay safe. Love, Mom." I send him packages once a week. Usually it's nothing more than some candy, newspapers, a magazine every so often, nuts and the like—anything that I think he'd like to get, like Oreos. He likes Nerds Ropes, so I try to send those along to him when I can find them in the store.

I dream about when he comes home in September. We'll make plans, go to dinner, go boating, play with the dogs, have a lot of fun, and just spend time together. I'm not thinking past September. I don't want to acknowledge that he'll go back to Iraq.

Finally, Dan was home from Baghdad for his mid-tour leave of eighteen days. He came home on September 10. We were able to go to the gate to greet him. I made a big poster that said, "Welcome Home Private Daniel C. White, Love, Mom, Dad, Rachel [his sister], Casey and Gracie [the dogs]." It was so exciting, waiting for him to deplane, and when we saw him, there were tears of joy and lots of hugs.

I took two full weeks off work to spend the time with him. It was a good visit. The first few days were an adjustment for both of us. I wanted him still to be my "little boy," while he was clearly a changed, grown man. After we adjusted to each other, we had a great visit.

I learned a lot about what he is doing in Baghdad. Probably more than I really want to know. I learned these things through conversations he would have with other people who were not afraid to know. Usually, an acquaintance of mine or my husband would ask him pointed questions about exactly what he is doing on a daily basis and Dan would answer honestly. I suppose he would have answered me the same if I had had the courage to ask. I learned that although he is trained as artillery, while he is in Baghdad, he and his platoon are serving as infantry. This means doing the patrols and searching for individuals who the Army feels should be detained. This equated to too much danger in my eyes—so I decided to focus on Dan, not on his duties. Dan and I went skydiving. It was the first time for both of us. It was a lot of fun and I think it was a great bonding experience.

The time flew by too quickly. Today we took Dan to the airport to begin his trip back to Baghdad to finish out his tour. He has four months remaining on his tour. This was a very difficult morning. When Dan awoke, he was different toward us. Not the same relaxed, smiling young man he had been for the past couple of weeks; he was already beginning to put on his "game face." When we arrived at the airport, our role as parents was to escort him to the gate and see him off.

I was touched that as we went through the metal detectors, one of the TSA workers handed Dan a baggie of candy for the trip. He extended his hand and said thanks to Dan as he offered him the bag of goodies. Of course, I began to get teary-eyed. I noticed many people in the concourse giving Dan a nod and a silent respectful thank-you.

When we got to the gate and waited for the plane, we stuck to "safe" topics and avoided any really "deep" conversations. There were two other soldiers at the gate waiting to go to Atlanta. One was Air Force and he was with his wife. The other was Army and he was with his girlfriend. As a mother, I felt very sad for the wife and girlfriend. When it was time for him to board the plane, I gave him a big hug, told him I loved him and to be safe, and started crying. His father gave him a hug and a strong handshake and told him he loved him and to be safe.

The other two soldiers were saying their goodbyes as well.

The husband and wife embraced, kissed, and said goodbye. The couple embraced, kissed, embraced, kissed, and embraced and kissed again to say goodbye. It was very sad to see young love being separated by the distance and the "job at hand," and I secretly prayed that they would make it through to continue their lives together.

Then we watched our son board and stayed to watch the plane take off. I stood by the window as he was getting on the plane. Dan looked for us at the window. I don't think he could see us because of the reflection, but I know that he knew we were there, watching and praying, and yes, crying.

I came to work this morning, have been here now for about three hours, and have done next to nothing. I don't feel like talking to people, I just want to be alone with my thoughts. Now I have to readjust to get back to being a strong mom for my son, and put on a brave face for strangers. The worry will soon creep back in, I'm sure. I'll go back to reading the paper each day to see what has happened the day before in Baghdad. I'll go back to sending weekly packages, notes of love and encouragement, and Oreos!

Most days I feel lucky. Thanks to the Internet and international calling cards, the mothers of today's war are so much better informed about their sons' well-being than mothers of prior wars. Yes, maybe we can find out too much, but at least we have some sense of calm when we get those e-mails or see the pictures, or just see the small purchases on the online bank account.

Karen White works as a community relations professional for KeyBank. She and her husband, Bob, have two adult children. Karen likes to paint and bake.

Acknowledgments

WITH HEARTFELT APPRECIATION, WE acknowledge family, friends, and colleagues for their steadfast support and encouragement:

Our brave young men and women in the military. We thank them for their selfless sacrifice and service to our country and pray for their safe return.

All of the mothers of soldiers who submitted stories for this project. Whether their stories appear in these pages or not, we are inspired by their love, dedication, and words from the heart.

Regina Brett, Cleveland *Plain Dealer* columnist and radio host, who gives people a voice to tell their stories. Her call for submissions helped gather these living histories.

Kristin Anderson, former Channel 3 WKYC reporter, who broadcast the first interview about our project.

Ray Rundelli, who generously gave of his time. His expert advice and counsel helped us understand the ins and outs of publishing contracts.

David Gray, our editor, Rob Lucas, our assistant editor, and Rosalie Wieder, our copy editor, who polished our work and made it shine.

Stan Edwin Mayer and Ed Reinart, our loving husbands, who believe in us.

All of our children: Stan Matthew, Anne Marie and Jason, Allie, and Tracy and Greg, Kristy and James, Katie and BJ, Meme and Matt, and Joseph for being our best cheerleaders. Thank you for your enthusiasm.

Stan Matthew Mayer and Joseph Reinart, our sons, who inspire us every day and whose military service moved us to do this project.

Janie also acknowledges:

Pat Kacsala, who has a beautiful spirit and loves what matters. Her thoughtful advice got the project rolling.

Mary Ryan, noted children's author, my mentor, who always takes the time. Her inspiration feeds my writing soul.

June Bolenbaugh, my National Writing Project partner. Her joy in writing is contagious and helps me find the words.

Eileen Davis, Priscilla Kaczuk, Bobbie Wason, and Sandra Philipson, my writing friends, who always, always encourage me.

Mary Anne also acknowledges:

Joanne Daly, who handed me an article written by Janie. Her kindness serendipitously sent us on our journey together.

The staff at St. Francis Xavier School in Medina, for nurturing us with their love and prayers.

Photo Credits

p. 15 (left), E.M. Kenneley; p. 15 (right), John Kenneley; p. 19, Edmund Reinart; p. 30, Stan Mayer; p. 36, David John McClaren; p. 40, Devon D. Dadich; p. 44, Jean Busch; p. 49, Daniel Lynch; p. 55, Mary Einwald; p. 66, David L. Swancer; p. 71, Darrell E. Fawley Jr.; p. 74, John Ross; p. 83, Mark Gebler; p. 88, Cliff Tengler; p. 92, Michael C. Hicks; p. 97, William E. Snow; p. 101, Ralph R. Burr Jr.; p. 104, Felix J. Goyetche; p. 110, Rudy Radva Sr.; p. 113, Paul Thomas Lang; p. 116, R. Wayne White; p. 118, Fred Berlin; p. 129, Richard E. Heaton; p. 135, Robin R. Siebenhar; p. 141, Robert Knight-Knight Studio; p. 147, Mark Gehri; p. 155, Melinda Paine; p. 159, Ed Redmond; p. 163, Kathryn McClellan; p. 168, Daniel R. Porter; p. 174, James M. Murawski; p. 176, Donald Walls; p. 191, Chris Norris; p. 195, Michael Estep; p. 199, Karen Phelps; p. 203, Gale Phelps; p. 207, Doug Anderson; p. 212, James M. Martin; p. 223, Robert T. White.

Your Own Story

For mothers of U.S. service men and women . . .

We believe that writing our stories helped us deal with the swirling emotions we felt during our children's deployment. The other mothers who contributed stories to this book agree.

Now, we invite you find out for yourself by writing your own story. You don't have to have any writing experience. You just have to be ready to open your heart.

You might select a beautiful journal and a favorite pen as your tools, or maybe a spiral notebook and pencil are more your style. Perhaps you're comfortable typing directly into a computer. Whatever tools you use, though, you'll want to find a quiet space and some time to write when you won't be interrupted.

You don't have to know exactly what you want to say when you begin. Just write. Let the words come from your mind and heart, down your arm to your hand and fingers, and let your thoughts flow on the page. Don't worry about spelling or grammar. Write without stopping all that is on your mind. Be prepared to shed some tears as you write. This process may take a few days, several weeks, or as long as you need.

Remember: the power of the story is in the detail.

Here are a few questions to get started:

- How did your everyday routines change when your child was deployed?
- What did you talk or write about with your son or daughter during deployment?

- What things did you do to cope with stress?
- How did the situation affect your relationship with your spouse?
- What surprised you most about the experience of having your child deployed in a war zone?
- How has this experience changed you?

When you've written everything you can think of in your journal and you have nothing left to add, you're ready for the next stage of writing: rewriting. And after that, you may decide that you're ready to share your story—with your child, your family, a church group, other mothers . . .

For tips on rewriting and sharing your story (including more examples of other mother's stories), visit our website at:

www.LoveYouMoreThanYouKnow.com

Now go sit down and get started—you'll be glad you did!